A CURE OF THE MIND

A CURE OF THE MIND

The Poetics of Wallace Stevens

Theodore Sampson

Montréal/New York
London

Black Rose Books No. CC280
Hardcover ISBN: 1-55164-149-6 (bound)
Paperback ISBN: 1-55164-148-8 (pbk.)

Canadian Cataloguing in Publication Data
Sampson, Theodore
A cure of the mind : the poetics of Wallace Stevens

Includes bibliographical references and index.
Hardcover ISBN: 1-55164-149-6 (bound)
Paperback ISBN: 1-55164-148-8 (pbk.)

1. Stevens, Wallace, 1879-1955--Criticism and interpretation.
I. Title.
PS3537.T4753Z7643 1999   811'.52   C99-900475-1

Cover image by Rhea Sampson
Cover design by Associés libres, Montréal

ιυυ

**BLACK
ROSE
BOOKS**

C.P. 1258
Succ. Place du Parc
Montréal, H2W 2R3
Canada

2250 Military Road
Tonawanda, NY
14150
USA

99 Wallis Road
London, E9 5LN
England
UK

To order books in North America:
(phone) 1-800-565-9523 (fax) 1-800-221-9985
In Europe: (phone) 0181-986-4854 (fax) 0181-533-5821

Our Web Site address: http://www.web.net/blackrosebooks
A publication of the Institute of Policy Alternatives of Montréal (IPAM)
Printed in Canada Le Conseil des Arts du Canada
The Canada Council for the Arts

CONTENTS

ON ABBREVIATIONS AND CITATIONS

CP   *The Collected Poems of Wallace Stevens* (New York: Alfred A. Knopf, 1954)

L   *Letters of Wallace Stevens*, selected and edited by Holly Stevens (New York: Alfred A. Knopf, 1981)

NA   *The Necessary Angel: Essays on Reality and the Imagination* (New York: Vintage Books, 1951)

OP   *Opus Posthumous*, edited by S.F. Morse (New York: Alfred A. Knopf, 1957)

PM   *The Palm at the End of the Mind*, edited by Holly Stevens (New York: Alfred A. Knopf, 1967)

SCB   *Sur Plusieurs Beaux Sujets: Wallace Stevens' Commonplace Book*, edited by Milton J. Bates (Stanford, California: Stanford University Press, 1989)

SP   *Souvenirs and Prophecies: The Young Wallace Stevens*, edited by Holly Stevens (New York: Alfred A. Knopf, 1977) *for Rhea, George, and Steph*

What inmost allegiance, what ultimate religion, would be proper to a wholly free and disillusioned spirit?

George Santayana

We live in the mind and poetry is a cure of the mind.

Wallace Stevens

Forget that passionate music. It will end.
True singing is a different breath, about
nothing. A gust inside a god. A wind.

Rainer Maria Rilke

The language cascades into the
invisible, beyond and above.

William Carlos Williams

To get *beyond poetry*, as Beethoven, in his later work, strove to get *beyond music*.

T. S. Eliot

PREFACE

In their attempt to cope with the awesome complexities of Stevens' 'metapoetic' verse embedded in his longer poems, the temptation among his critics and literary theorists in general—I have in mind Harold Bloom—is to devise their own grid of critical precepts which they then proceed to apply in their analysis of Stevens' mind and poetry. Needless to say, the fatal drawback in such a procedure is that eventually the critic's theorizations tend to compound Stevens' own inherent obscurities, so that the entire operation only adds to the existing postmodernist blur, or what now passes as meaningful critical discourse. The only solution, then, in dealing with Stevens' complex mind and poetry is to meet them squarely on their own ground; and in so doing, to rely only on one's critical sense, having as a guide whatever clues or insights are available in the canon itself.

Thus, as Hillis Miller wisely warns us, "The critic must resign himself to the poet's world and accept what he finds there";[1] which means that the only reliable venue to the tangents of Stevens' poetic complexity is to be found in the intricate workings of his own mind, since "the multiple meanings" and the involuted verbal music that emerge from Stevens' verse are, in the final analysis, "tangents of himself."[2] As Roland Bush observes in discussing Eliot's own poetic idiom—and his observation applies to Stevens' sensibility as well—we cannot begin to fathom his [Eliot's] "modernist dialectic between music and dialogue stripped of outside reference. . .unless we understand the internal pressures he lives with."[3] In choosing, however, this method of reading Stevens' poetry one is bound to

ix

leave oneself completely open to the charge of `phenomenological fallacy'; but then, one is no longer inclined to take such labels seriously since, as Geoffrey Hartman impishly points out, literary criticism has now become "a contemporary form of theology,"[4] so that what ultimately counts in our approach to Stevens' poetry is the degree to which subject and method are felicitously married.

In the course of my own efforts to delve into Stevens' poetic mind, that is, in trying to find a plausible reason for the way he conceives and writes his poems, I have used as guidelines what I consider to be a number of fundamental quetions which over the years his critics have either not cared to ask, have only partially answered, or chosen to be mute about. The questions are as follows: (a) "Why does Stevens engage in such play?"[5] Or, better put, why this insatiable desire to express even the most ordinary impressions, feelings, and perceptions in rationally incomprehensible poetic tropes, as if—in Charles Olson's words—"One perception must immediately and directly lead to a further perception. . .keep moving, keep in speed?"[6] (b) What does Stevens really mean when he says that "The poet speaks the poem as it is" (CP 473), and to what extent does such a practice connote a solipsistic conception of poetry? (c) And again, what does Stevens mean by such sliding phrases as "The poem of the mind" and "the act of the mind" (CP 239, 240) and to what extent do such phrases further intimate a solipsistic poetics? (d) Also, if what he calls "the spirit's alchemicana" (CP 471) addresses itself to the irrational element in poetry, to what extent is such an element dominant in his theory and practice of poetry, and therefore in what way is Stevens' intricate verbal music dependent on his irrational use of language—a "pure rhetoric of a language without words?" (CP 374). And finally, in summarizing these questions, the one most crucial question: is Stevens' use of the poetic act purely aesthetic, and if so, to what extent is it used as a means for attaining an ontological renewal or higher elevation of the self?

In undertaking to answer some of these questions in my treatise, I have deliberately eschewed lengthy analyses of Stevens' longer poems, with the exception of "An Ordinary Evening in New Haven" which constitutes a test-case for my central argument in this book. The reason I have avoided doing so is because, in the final analysis, all of Stevens' long poems are beyond interpretation; in the sense that they are so totally open-ended in theme, structure, and language that they cannot be said to offer a definite rational meaning to the reader. As Frank Lentricchia correctly points out, when reading poetry of such complexity, we are confronted with a "series of networks of interrelation whose connections and boundaries are not securable because they are ruled by never-ending movements of linguistic energy."[7] I have, however, as a kind of compensation, made every effort to discuss and clarify a number of crucial points in the canon that are still pending a final interpretation or valid elucidation, as is the case with "Not Ideas about the Thing but the Thing Itself." I would like to believe that my analysis of this poem will absolve me from all my sins of omission in this book.

NOTES

1. *Poets of Reality: Six Twentieth-Century Writers* (New York: Atheneum Books, 1969), p.291.

2. M.L. Rosenthal, "Stevens as Hedonist, Pluralist and Platonist," in *Wallace Stevens: The Critical Heritage*, ed. Charles Doyle (London: Routledge and Kegan Paul, 1985), p.309.

3. T.S. Eliot: *A Study in Character and Style* (New York: Oxford University Press, 1985), pp.xii, xiii.

4. *Criticism in the Wilderness: The Study of Literature Today* (New Haven and London: Yale University Press, 1980), p.54.

5. Alan Perlis, *Wallace Stevens: A World of Transforming Shapes* (Lewisburg: Bucknell University Press, 1976), p.24.

6. Quoted in Marjorie Perloff, *The Futurist Moment: Avant-Garde, Avant Guerre, and the Language of Rupture* (Chicago and London: The University of Chicago Press, 1986), p.23.

7. *After the New Criticism* (Chicago: The University of Chicago Press, 1980), p. 189. As Hillis Miller puts it in even more dramatic or `deconstructive' terms, in each one of Stevens' long poems "There is always a remainder, something alogical left over that does not fit any logical scheme of interpretation . . .Its textual richness opens abyss beneath abyss, beneath each deep a deeper deep, as the reader interrogates its elements and lets each question generate an answer that is another question in its turn. *Each question opens another distance, a perspective begun as A that begins again at B, without ever reaching any closer to the constantly receding horizon*. Such a poem is incapable of being encompassed in a single logical formulation. It calls forth potentially endless commentaries, each one of which, like this essay, can only formulate and reformulate the poem's receding abysses. The linguistic momentum of the poem generates a corresponding momentum in commentaries on the poem" (emphasis mine). See *The Linguistic Moment: From Wordsworth to Stevens* (Princeton, N.J.: Princeton University Press, 1985), pp.409, 422. Miller's valuation of Stevens' longer poems provides the theoretical matrix for my central argument in this book.

CHAPTER I

Stevens' Poetic Mind

> The mind is the end and must be satisfied.
>
> Wallace Stevens,
> "Extracts from Addresses to the Academy of Fine Ideas"

1

A man whose desire is "To live in the world but outside existing conceptions of it" (*OP* 164) and who, as a poet, takes to "musing the obscure" (*CP* 88) by "The extension of the mind beyond the range of the mind," and "the projection of reality beyond reality" (*NA* 171), obviously sets for both himself and his reader an impossible task. The task is impossible in the sense that the ideal reader, who as a critic is temperamentally given to the habit of reading and interpreting verse in rational terms, when confronted with poetry written on such tenuous or unreal premises, he is naturally bound to be overcome by its precious obscurities.[1] In other words, having tried stubbornly to make sense of the work of a poet who, among other things, "requires of it a meaning beyond what its words can say" (*OP* 210), the reader finally realizes that the poems he has so assiduously read, eventually turn out to be nothing less than "labyrinths" that have no exit.[2] Nevertheless, nothing is completely lost; in the end, and after having taken honest stock of his inadequacies as a critic, he is consoled by the thought that he has at least been able to delve into the depths, and taken the true measure of that intractable poetic voice for what it really is:

1

A Cure of the Mind

[S]omething unpredictable, savage, violent, without ascertainable cause or explanation, irrational, as he said genuine poetry must be. It is both a voice and a way of writing. It is something continuous, murmuring or muttering, sometimes a singsong rhyme or a stammering alliteration. Continuously present in his work, it is nevertheless a principle of discontinuity. It forbids explication by sources. It breaks into the formal order of both thought and shapely poetry. This voice appears intermittently and faintly even in Stevens' earliest journals and poems.[3]

Needless to say, when faced with poetry that flaunts its complexity to such a degree, and having accepted the impossibility of ever hoping to find in it—as is the case with Stevens—"a single systematic theory of poetry and life,"[4] then there is only one crucial question that the critic needs ask himself: "We want to know where that poetry comes from and how we should read it."[5] In answering this momentous question, and given the impossibility of a commonly agreed upon Stevens poetics, the only way to find out `where that poetry comes from' and how we should read it, lies in our ability to locate and define the source and nature of Stevens' discontinuities[6] resting at the center of his intricate poetic mind. I further believe that this alternative route to Stevens' poetry is intrinsically challenging for the critic, because Stevens' poetic disjunctions have never been fully explored or given a satisfactory theoretical explanation by any of his major critics and commentators.[7] It is my firm belief, then, that if we are able to identify the true meaning of Stevens' discontinuities, that is map out the perimeters of his poetic mind and find its true pulse—what *it is that impels his mind to poetic creation*—then we should definitely be in a better position to tell `where that poetry comes from' and thus be able to read it with greater assurance, understanding, and ease.

2

In their attempt over the years to find a way to read Stevens' poetry, his critics have, as a rule, opted for one of two following approaches: (a) to try to focus and enlarge upon one of Stevens' main poetic ideas[8] as the thematic pivot in a number of his major poems; or (b) apply a predetermined or ready-made theory to his work as a whole,[9] and then proceed to use such a theory as a general critical matrix in their discussion and analysis of individual poems. In both cases, the tendency is to try and expand their chosen approach or theory into an all-encompassing poetics applicable to Stevens' thought and poetry. Their intentions, however, are invariably betrayed mainly because the theories they formulate and apply either fail to come to grips with the complexity of Stevens' mind, or give a plausible explanation for the essentially irrational—or better, alogical—nature of his poetic tropes and figurations.[10] Finally, what his critics manage to achieve, in the best of cases, is a sort of subpoetics which could not be said to provide the student of Stevens' poetry with a reliable guide for glossing its difficulties, and in the process help him find out `where it comes from' and learn `how to read it'. I firmly believe that this is where the true challenge lies in our efforts to read and understand Stevens' poetry—a challenge which, as Hillis Miller points out, remains unanswered to this day. I further believe that the study of Stevens' major poetic ideas—'decreation', `first idea', `center', `fictions', `chaos and nonthingness',—as exegetical matrices for an understanding of either Stevens' mind or poetry, can lead us nowhere. What we want really to discover and identify is the source and true timbre of Stevens' voice—how and why it generates and articulates, through poetic language, its intricate meanings; and in order to find the source of that voice, we definitely have to look for it elsewhere.

3

As a poet, Stevens was as much addicted to abstract ideas as he was to writing poetry every single day of his life.[11] Drawn irresistibly to what one of his critics calls "the concept-forging fecundity of the human intellect,"[12] Stevens liked to believe that "Ideas are all we have"—implying that the only true reality extant are the poetic and philosophic conceptualizations we create out of our life experiences—and at a certain point he even convinces himself that "the abstract is as immanent in the mind of the poet, as the idea of God is immament in the mind of the theologian" (L 434). We must, however, always be on our guard whenever confronted with such assertions on Stevens' part, and therefore be prepared to qualify them accordingly.

A man with an unusually strong but highly volatile mind given to constant vacillation and self-contradiction, Stevens' attraction to a given idea is as immediate and unqualified as is his final rejection of it. In other words, he admires or accepts an idea not on the basis of its intrinsic intellectual efficacy, depth, or lasting truth, but for its potential usefulness as poetic material.[13] As he makes it quite clear in his essay "A Collect of Philosophy," what attracts him primarily to philosophic ideas is their "poetic nature," the fact that the conceptual and poetic modes of human perception are, for him, closely affined since, each in its own unique way, "transforms reality" creatively—which is why, for Stevens, "Poets and philosophers often think alike" (OP 183,185,186).[14] However, for Stevens the true ground of this close affinity between the poetic and the conceptual is the common integrative effect they have on the

4

mind; because according to him, both the analytic intellect and the poetic imagination ultimately "probe(s) for an integration," except that poetry achieves its `integrations' through its imaginative "insight [and] evocative power" (*OP* 196).[15]

As a necessary corrective against the impression one might have of Stevens as being overly receptive to ideas in general, it should be mentioned that at times of intense inner crisis, he is actually opposed to them. At heart a transcendental monist thinly disguised as a "connoisseur of chaos" (*CP* 215), and therefore constantly in search for a unitive vision of life—"the diamond pivot bright" and "bright *scienza*" (*CP* 207,248) "beyond this present knowing" (*OP* 101)—Stevens knows only too well that "The law of chaos is the law of ideas" (*CP* 255); the fact that an inordinate amount of conceptualizing about life betrays a spiritually restless and discontented mind. And this crucial insight is born of Stevens' bleaker, more reductive moments, when he becomes conscious of "The dominant blank, the unapproachable" that "underlies all trials of device" (*CP* 477): his devastating perception that all of man's myths, ideas, and beliefs, created out of his ceaseless struggle for inner unity, eventually turn into the grey ash of spiritual disillusion.[16] Thus, though they may be said to augment poetic feeling and an imaginative response to life, in the end these ideas also become a manifestation of man's inner disunity. Born of man's need to create order out of the chaotic flux of life, ideas eventually become part of the chaos they seek to contain. And so, as a quester seeking that `diamond pivot bright', and as an aggrieved monist deprived of "the grandeur of a total edifice" (*CP* 511), Stevens needs to warn us that "The structure of ideas, these ghostly sequences/Of the mind, result only in disaster" (*CP* 326).

There is, however, one among Stevens' many poetic ideas which could be said to provide an authentic basis for a comprehensive poetics of both his mind and work, and this is the concept of what he himself chooses to call "the reality-imagination complex."[17] This is a pivotal idea that lies at the heart of Stevens' poetic sensibility and work, and what needs to be said about it is that the very conflict involved in this `complex'—the opposition between the imaginative and the real, the transcendent and the earth-bound—has its roots in Stevens' own inner division, in "a war between the mind/And sky. . ./a war that never ends" (CP 407); the fact that one part of his mind "is committed to the brute substance of earth, things as they are, and the other just as tenaciously searches out such majesty as it can find."[18]

In one of his major essays, "The Noble Rider and the Sound of Words," Stevens provides us with the best single text for glossing this conflict, and also for elucidating further upon a significant aspect of his own mind. He frames his central argument by contending that what he calls "the pressure of reality" or "things as they are" (NA 16,25)—be it the prevailing socio-political conditions, the general tenor of the times, or some deeper ontological crisis—tends to encroach upon our consciousness to such a degree as to overpower the mind and threaten to deprive it of its "power of contemplation" (NA 20)—that is, of its capacity for free and spontaneous poetic creation; and if this possibility does become a reality, then it will mean the death of the imagination. Thus involved in a ceaseless war with `things as they are', the mind must be prepared at all times, through the power of poetic metaphor, to counterpose reality's pressure with a counterpressure of its own; and in so doing, it will not only keep reality at bay, but also prove imagination's incontestable sway over it.

As dramatized in his poetry, the imagination-reality conflict constitutes one of Stevens' major themes as well as his most potent source of inspiration since, by constantly attracting and mobilizing his mind through its endless, dynamic tensions,

6

it accounts for his most characteristic and powerful verse. And yet, as pervasive and central as this conflict may be in the canon, it eventually tells us very little about `where the poetry comes from' or how we should read it. It does, however, bring to surface another and more essential facet of Stevens' sensibility: an ingrained perspectivist dimension of mind that lies at a deeper layer of his poetic consciousness, of which the imagination-reality complex is only an aesthetic by-product. As Hillis Miller perceptively points out in his general assessment of Stevens' poetry, "all his work is an attempt to explore the endlessly variable perspectives from which reality can be viewed by the imagination."[19] The kind of perspectivism Miller has in mind goes beyond such exemplary genre pieces as "Metaphor of a Magnifico" (*CP* 19), "Thirteen Ways of Looking at a Blackbird" (*CP* 92), "Sea Surface Full of Clouds" (*CP* 98), as well as those poems marked for their extreme obscurity of theme and language, and whose involuted meaning ultimately resides in Stevens' own mind. It is, therefore, necessary to try and locate the source of Stevens' poetic perspectivism, and then proceed to delineate and relate its crucial relevance to his work as a whole.[20]

The modern perspectivist mind has its beginnings in the American empiricist philosophers and Nietzsche's own radical `transvaluations of values' or sweeping rejection of all `truths':

> *The feeling of valuelessness is attained when one apprehends that the world fails to have in the plenitude of happenings any overreaching unity; and therefore the character of existence is not `true' is false. . .One has no longer any ground to persuade himself of a true world.*[21]

As a consequence, in the absence of a cohering center—the old "categories of `purpose', `oneness', and `being' "[22]—reality is reduced to "a raging chaos of particulars which cannot be authentically synthesized. . .because there is no unifying ground

7

for such a synthesis";[23] and what is more, the corollary to such a fragmented vision of the world is that our perception or understanding of reality becomes "open to an endless series of new interpretations."[24] It is exactly at this point that the modern perspectivist mind is born: amidst the wreckage of an older, stable worldview with all its epistemological props knocked from under it, since in the wake of universal confusion "There is no truth, only interpretations of it";[25] thus, individual perception of reality *perforce* becomes a "chaos of sensations."[26]

There is, however, another and equally significant component in the modern perspectivist's emerging worldview, and this is the new model of the physical universe created by the mathematical formulas of twentieth-century physicists. According to the physical laws of relativity, the idea of the world as something fixed and eternal, determined by "an accumulation of categories, abstract concepts and general laws," is no longer tenable and must therefore be abolished; instead we must see the universe for what it really is: "an infinitely complex lattice of relationships"[27] as prescribed by Bergson's *ensemble de relations absolues*," Whitehead's "manifold of prehensions," and Ortega y Gasset's *perspectivismo*.[28] In postulating his own perspectivist theory on the basis of Einsteinian physics, Ortega argues that the notion of an absolute single truth—or what once was held to be *the* truth—must now be replaced by the view of reality as "a complex of multiple truths," with the added corollary that the emerging plurality or diversity of such truths in no way invalidates their separate, individual truth.[29] It is, however, Emerson, the American progenitor of modern perspectivism, who posits human sight as a trope for the proliferation of individual truths; the fact that truth is not only contigent upon the `inner eye,' but that truth so conceived consists of a series of `circles' or perspectives, receding into infinite space:

8

The eye is the first circle; the horizon which it forms is the second; and throughout nature this primary figure is repeated without end. . .Our life is an apprenticeship to the truth that around every circle another can be drawn; that there is no end in nature, that every end is a beginning; that there is always another dawn risen on mid-noon, and under every deep a lower deep opens.[30]

Thus, to the modern perspectivist's shocking revelation of reality as "a dissolving, a blending, a merging of things. . .mutually exclusive," is now added the supreme challenge of having to comprehend and give meaning to a world reduced to a boundless, impersonal system of infinite subtruths or perspectives.[31]

Such a perspectivism as outlined here, depicting a fragmented and fluid world governed solely by myriad random objects floating aimlessly in an unstable and centerless universe, and wherein the mind feels and thinks in a similar manner—this constitutes the perspectivist master image of self and world that lies at the heart of Stevens' mind and poetry. One of his most characteristic poems, appropriately entitled "Chaos in Motion and Not in Motion," is a telling allegory of the modern mind as seen from a purely perspectivist angle. Assuming a mock-heroic tone, Stevens proceeds to depict his protagonist's disarrayed mind as a phenomenological mélange of totally incongruous incidents, emblematic of his befuddled mental landscape. Stevens' primary intention in this poem is to give us an intimate, dramatized version of his protagonist's disordered consciousness[32] as an inner projection of outer chaos:

Oh, that this lashing wind was something more
Than the spirit of Ludwig Richter. . .

The rain is pouring down. It is July.
There is lightning and the thickest thunder.

9

A Cure of the Mind

It is a spectacle. Scene 10 becomes 11,
In series X, Act IV, et cetera.

People fall out of windows, trees tumble down,
Summer is changed to winter, the young grow old,
The air is full of children, statues, roofs
And snow. The theatre is spinning around,
Colliding with deaf-mute churches and optical
                                   [trains.

The most massive sopranos are singing songs of
                                   [scales.
And Ludwig Richter, turbulent Schlemihl,
Has lost the whole in which he was contained,
Knows desire without an object of desire,
All mind and violence and nothing left.

He knows he has nothing more to think about,
Like the wind that lashes everything at once.
                    (CP 357-58)

For Ludwig Richter, the poem's hero-perspectivist[33] who `Has lost the whole in which he was contained' and now lives in the modern physicists' "directionless space of infinite nothingness,"[34] reality has no longer any order or solid structure other than the flux of discrete, empirical particulars, nor a fixed standpoint from which the mind could survey the physical universe as an organic whole. So Richter is aggrieved by the knowledge that "the sky is divested of its fountains" (*CP* 321), which to him now is "a facade for nothingness,"[35] and that the place where "There was a heaven once" (*OP* 53) has now turned itself into a "skeleton of the ether" (*CP* 443).[36] As for time, it too has

10

become an agent that augments and perpetuates the chaotic flux of things—a flux that has no beginning nor end:

> *Like water running in the gutter*
> *Through an alley to nowhere,*
> *Without beginning or the concept of an end.*
> (OP 76)

And what was once for him the eternal truth of things, has now been shattered to pieces and lies in his mind as "a litter of truths" (CP 216):

> *"There is no such thing as truth,"*
>
> ....
>
> *"There are many truths,*
> *But they are not parts of a truth."*
> (CP 203)

But even more shattering is Richter's insight that man has lost for ever the urge to create or believe in new mythopoetic conceptions of self and world, because any such truth would only prove to be

> *Just one more truth, one more*
> *Element in the immense disorder of truths.*
> (CP 216)

And so, in Richter's fragmented mind, what was once the solid structure of a stable and fixed world, has now been replaced by the apocalyptic sight of that selfsame world crumbling into ruins:

> *Parts of the immense detritus of a world*
> *That is completely waste, that moves from waste*
> *To waste, out of the hopeless waste of the past*
> *Into a hopeful waste to come.* (OP 49)

The bitterly ironic and devastating thrust of the final line—`a hopeful waste to come'—shows the extent of Richter's grief over the loss of his inner unity, as well as his bleak certainty that he will never again know such unity. And because he is `All mind and violence and nothing left,/He knows he has nothing more to think about,' and as a result his mind is `Like the wind that lashes everything at once.'[37] Finally, following his inner collapse, whereby his former sense of the world as something stable and meaningful has now become "a moving chaos that never ends" (*OP* 50), Richter's rudderless mind appears to revert to a primeval state where it identifies with the universal flux of things:

> *We live in a constellation*
> *Of patches and pitches,*
> *Not in a single world,*
>
> ....
>
> *Thinkers without final thoughts*
> *In an always incipient cosmos.*
>   (*OP* 114-15)

`*Thinkers without final thoughts*': this describes perfectly the inner vacuum that impels Crispin, Stevens' arch-perspectivist and primary persona, to embark on his momentous and agonizing quest for a new viable aesthetic and reality-model, what he chooses to call "the fecund minimum" or "veritable ding an sich" (*CP* 29,35). But more significantly, it would be a search in the course of which Crispin the quester-perspectivist will give birth to a new self: the experimental poet-aesthete who out of his tortured, disarrayed phenomenology will fashion for himself a radically new idiom which would eventually be the breaking ground for Stevens' own `savage' and `irrational' poetic voice.[38]

4

Starting out as a post-empiricist, living in "a world of chaotic mutation"[39] now reduced to a "cadaverous Eden" (*OP* 61) and a heap of "dreadful sundry" (*CP* 47), Crispin is Stevens' paradigmatic perspectivist-comedian; a man who, impelled by his "rage for order" (*CP* 130) and the need to recover the lost `center'[40] of his shattered world, turns himself into a poet-errant.[41] In "Landscape with Boat," a real tour de force of reductive introspection, Stevens recreates through the use of striking and vivid imagery the struggle of Crispin's mind, as it tries to find its way back to the penetralium or truth of things—the `ding an sich' of reality:

> *He brushed away the thunder, then the clouds,*
> *Then the colossal illusion of heaven. Yet still*
> *The sky was blue. He wanted imperceptible air.*
> *He wanted to see. He wanted the eye to see*
> *And not be touched by blue. He wanted to know,*
> *A naked man who regarded himself in the glass*
> *Of air, who looked for the world beneath the blue,*
> *Without blue, without any turquoise tint or phase,*
> *Any azure under-side or after-color. Nabob*
> *Of bones, he rejected, he denied, to arrive*
> *At the neutral centre, the ominous element,*
> *The single-colored, colorless, primitive.*
> (*CP* 241-42)

In actual fact, the poem has a double thematic thrust to it: not only does it reenact the empiricist's fierce inner drive to strip the world down to its empirical essentials in his obsessive quest for the true `center' of things, but it also understates Crispin's poignant discovery that the center he had been searching for,

13

eventually turns out to be `colorless', `neutral', and `primitive'; that is to say, a mere illusion or convenient mental fiction.

This act of radical self-introspection as described in "Landscape with Boat"[42] provides us with the best gloss for understanding the true meaning of Crispin's inner odyssey, and in particular the grim epistemological and aesthetic impasse in which he finds himself. An inveterate *post mortem Dei*[43] perspectivist or endlessly improvising poetaster in search of both a `soul' and a new aesthetic, whose mind is lost in "a multiplicity of perspectives"[44] and "released from any clear sense of itself,"[45] Crispin's voyage is a comedy that often verges on the tragic.[46] Suspended in a spiritual limbo and living "In a world without a plan" (*OP* 76) or "imagination" (*CP* 27), his tortuous quest ends with the painful realization that there is no `truth' and that "all things [are] the truth" (*CP* 242). This insight has such a shattering effect on him that it causes his every new epistemological discovery or poetic revelation to end in disaster; a fact that only deepens his crisis and brings his mind close to the brink of total collapse.[47] Crispin's persistent crisis derives from the fact that he has allowed his mind to be caught in a vicious stalemate it cannot break; in other words, he is unable to reintegrate his consciousness simply because he cannot make whole again the world without.[48] As a result, he perpetually flounders amidst a rushing flood of stray perceptions, poetic illuminations, and ineffectual epistemological speculations, causing his sense of self and world to remain up to the very end fluidly structureless and unstable.[49]

There is, however, a profound inward experience that Crispin goes through at the end of his disastrous journey, a kind of `inner leap' which clearly indicates that he is finally turning from a hapless, disoriented perspectivist and casual versifier, to a serious poet on the verge of a new and vital poetic idiom. Proceeding on the wise precept that an "uncentered self can hardly be anything than continuing drama and conflict,"[50] he accepts the inescapable fact that "Impermanence is the only permanence,"[51] and that it is "only in multiple perspectives [that] the world becomes real."[52] From this knowledge, he proceeds to the second momentous discovery, namely that the absolute `truth' or `center' of things is to be found in the random, empirical `truths' or `finite centers' of our fragmented consciousness.[53] The far-reaching implications of this last revelation is that truth does not only rest in our immediate empirical experiences and perceptions, but also in the immanence of the myriad of things in this world that make up our consciousness. In the concluding lines of "The Comedian as the Letter C" we are given a sketchy but revealing self-portrait of Crispin the newly-born poet, which could also very well serve as his poetic manifesto:

> *Prone to distemper he abates in taste,*
> *Fickle and fumbling, variable, obscure,*
> *Glozing his life with after-shining flicks,*
> *Illuminating, from a fancy gorged*
> *By apparition, plain and common things.*
>   (CP 46)

As such, it seems to offer an aesthetic that can be best summed up by two of Stevens' most characteristic poetic aphorisms and beliefs: "Reality is the spirit's true center," and "In the long run the truth does not matter" (*OP* 177,180).[54]

In fact, the final two lines of the quatrain cited above—'Illuminating, from a fancy gorged/By apparition, plain and common things'—provide the best single gloss for an understanding of the poetic idiom informing *Harmonium* as a whole; an idiom that has its historical roots in the radical and revitalizing `splendor-in-the-grass' aesthetic of the English Romantic poets, and which was to be adopted later by the twentieth-century modernist poets as an essential part of their own doctrine and poetic practice.[55] As Albert Gelpi correctly observes, it is a poetic whose primary aim is to rediscover the lost "spiritual forms and energies" of an "otherwise fragmented phenomenal world," and by so doing, to invest it with a new and "exalted coherence."[56] But in order to achieve this momentous goal, the mind needs first to overcome the brute immanence of empirical reality; and this it can only do by proceeding to reclaim "the sheer ontological weight and depth of the world,"[57] in Hopkins' marvellous phrase, "the dearest freshness deep down things."[58] In other words, what this new idiom demands from the poet is that he must pay heed to the quiddities of ordinary things, to their "elementary *haecceitas*, that particularity which is felt in *this* `red wheelbarrow glazed with rain water'," and nothing else.[59] Finally, as a new, ground-breaking poetic idiom rigorously engaged in rediscovering and recapturing the vital primacy of things, and doing so in a way whereby the phenomenal and the noumenal become interchangeable—the key phrase in the quatrain is `illuminating plain and common things'—it enlarges the scope of imaginative perception and allows for bold experimentation in both form and theme. More significantly, however, it unifies the poet's sensibility by fusing, within the strict confines of the poetic act, all contraries of thought and feeling so that the mind, now perfectly equipoised and free, may experience

> the strong exhilaration
> Of what we feel from what we think, of thought
> Beating in the heart, as if blood newly came,
> An elixir, an excitation, a pure power.
> (CP 382)

But there is a deeper reason for this impassioned acceptance of ordinary objects as *materia poetica*—born out of the phrase already cited: `illuminating plain and common things'—and alluded to by Coleridge in *Biographia Literaria*:

> *Poetry must give the charm of novelty to things of every day, and* to excite a feeling analogous to the supernatural, *by awakening the mind's attention from the lethargy of custom, and directing it to the loveliness and the wonders of the world* (emphasis mine).[60]

According to M. H. Abrams, the Romantics' radically revised concept of poetry not only initiated a major shift in literary sensibility but also created, by the very nature of such a shift, what he calls a "religio-aesthetic dimension" in Anglo-American literature.[61] What Abrams' telling phrase specifically refers to are the quasi-religious patterns of thought and feeling, particularly those derived from Christian theology, that helped to determine and shape some of the major themes of Victorian literature; in fact to such an extent that two of its most prominent and publicized authors could unabashedly declare, in open defiance of the new scientific ethos, that "dull. . .despised things are an Epiphany of God," and that "through every grass-blade. . .the glory of a present God still beams."[62] As Abrams goes on to argue, this `dimension' of nineteenth-century literature and all it connotes, became part of the poetic sensibility and vocabulary of most twentieth-century modernists, whose characteristic work, despite the thick overlay of aesthetic doctrine, is marked by a strong urge to try and discover the supersensible in the sensible, the transcendent in the immanent, the profane in the holy. In other words, the modernist poets seem to be impelled by a consuming desire to convert their poetic perceptions into an act of spiritual apprehension; and they do so by engaging themselves in endless "doxological relfections [on] the final goodness of things," seeking to turn them into "objects of faith,"[63] or, in the words of Frederick Hoffman, into a kind of "surrogate divinity."[64] And this desire, in its moments of highest intensity or inner depth, is quite often expressed in overly religious terms: "All objects demand to be seen" and, with a "new consciousness and perception gained, they must be christened anew, baptized, as it were, into a new Church."[65] We eventually come to see the true meaning of this `religio-aesthetic dimension', which is the modern artist's profound urge to find, amid the endless and trivial minutiae of daily life, "the ineluctable modality of the invisible";[66] that is, the noumenal in the phenomenal, and which he then can experience as something `analogous to the supernatural'. But what is more, we also come to realize that this seemingly aesthetic need to epiphanize the brute immanence of things[67]—be it through Emerson's `inner light', Rimbaud's `illuminations', Joyce's `epiphanies', Pound's `luminous details', or Stevens' "moments of the classic, the beautiful" (*OP* 112)—points to only one thing: the modern poet's supreme task of providing, through his art, a buffer between ourselves and the outer darkness or void that surrounds us.[68]

5

The Stevensian perspectivist that finally emerges in *Harmonium* is equipped with a new and vital poetic which offers him "the austere satisfaction of a self dependent on the pure poetry of the physical world"; and as such, it is a poetic that is marked by a purely aesthetic attitude towards life.[69] At heart still a `disoriented voyager without a haven,' but who has come to terms with his fragmented sense of self and world, he nevertheless refuses to pose either as a quasi-mystical Symbolist who accepts "the close interrelation of the physical and spiritual as an evident fact,"[70] or as a hard-headed nominalist who believes that "Each thing has its own particularity," and therefore must always try to "put the mind within the life of objects."[71] As a self-avowed empiricist, his mind seduced by the chaotic but creatively exhilarating disorder of the physical world, Stevens' poet-perspectivist abandons himself to its inexhaustible diversity, color, energy, and sensuous glories; what he calls in moments of ecstacy, "This present,/This *vif*, this dizzle-dazzle of being new/And of becoming, [this] air of freshness, clearness, greeness, and blueness" (*CP* 530).[72] And if, at times, he feels impelled to believe in "the dream of a magical universe,"[73] he must do so on the basis of his fidelity to the physical world and the fecund poetic perceptions born out of such fidelity. In other words, he must not, at all costs, try to extract a spiritual meaning from `the ineluctable modality of the visible' (poetic symbolism), or make an effort to read such meaning into the brute, opaque immanence of the physical universe (poetic nominalism).[74]

In his essay on "On Poetic Truth,"[75] Stevens starts out by acknowledging that there is "a unity rooted in the individuality of objects" that we should, as poets, try and "establish some communion with"; however, in the course of his discussion, he hastens to add that "a thing is what it is," and that it is only by "a quickening of our [poetic] awareness" that an object becomes `real'—a process which, according to him, "is the very soul of art" (*OP* 236,237). In other words, like a traditional `logocentrist' or non-nominalist, Stevens firmly believes that the true essence or substance of a thing—its *whatness*—does not lie in its material integrity but in the `word' itself, that is, in poetic troping or metaphor. He makes his position on this issue quite clear in "The Noble Rider and the Sound of Words," where he states conclusively that "A poet's words are of things that do not exist without the words" (*NA* 32).

"Local Objects,"[76] a poem written in the last year of Stevens' life (1955), doubtlessly constitutes a final and valid

19

summation of his lifelong commitment to the things of this world, and his artistic use of them as poetic material:

> *He knew that he was a spirit without a foyer*
> *And that, in this knowledge, local objects become*
> *More precious than the most precious objects of home:*
>
> *The local objects of a world without a foyer,*
> *Without a remembered past, a present past,*
> *Or a present future, hoped for in present hope,*
>
> *Objects not present as a matter of course,*
> *On the dark side of the heavens or the bright,*
> *In that sphere with so few objects of its own.*
>
> *Little existed for him but for the few things*
> *For which a fresh name always occurred, as if*
> *He wanted to make them, keep them from perishing,*
>
> *The few things, the objects of insight, the integrations*
> *Of feeling, the things that came of their own accord,*
> *Because he desired without quite knowing what,*
>
> *That were the moments of the classic, the beautiful.*
> *These were that serene he had always been approaching*
> *As towards an absolute foyer beyond romance.*
>   (OP 111-12)

Obviously the poet is mourning the absence of a guiding faith both in his own personal life and in the desacralized modern world at large; as a consequence, he looks upon the things of this earth as articles of a `surrogate divinity', vessels that contain what we once held to be sacred.[77] However, individual objects as such, particularly those that are tethered to our creaturely or daily existence, can only move us in an aesthetic way, since we respond to them intuitively by giving them a `fresh name', in itself a process that helps us `integrate' our feelings (art's supreme task). Furthermore, the meanings that accrue from things written about as `objects of insight,' are by necessity contingent upon the poet's intuitions, perceptions or mood; that is, meanings that come of `their own accord' and therefore fortuitous, since the perspectivist writes his poems `without quite knowing' what it is that he `desires'. According to Stevens, a poet's `absolute foyer', in an aesthetic sense, should not be found in his celebration of the primacy or quiddity of things, but in his intense, imaginative effort to experience them as `moments of the classic, the beautiful', `the serene.'[78]

A number of critics apparently are confused or uncertain about the true aesthetic nature or function of material objects in Stevens' poetry. For example, George S. Lensing believes that "for Stevens, the persistent and elusive quest for the mind's harmonious encounter with external objects. . .was antecedent to all other human interests"—a valuation which fails to identify the exact relation of poetic objects to Stevens' sensibility.[79] For Stevens, a poet's primary aim should not be the `harmonious encounter' with empirical particulars as these enter our consciousness, but the strong intuitive effort to try and extract as much aesthetic emotion from such particulars as possible, and in so doing—in the actual process of writing actual poems—experience such emotions as `integrations of feeling.' In other words, for Stevens the poet, the initial experience of things as poetic objects must eventually lead to a deepening integration of consciousness and not to the discovery of an object's supposedly numinous quiddity.[80] As Newton Stallknecht points out in his perceptive study of "The Man with the Blue Guitar," "The poet (Stevens) is not concerned primarily with things as they are but with his own consciousness."[81] On the other hand,

Helen Vendler in her reading of "Local Objects,"after making the valid observation that, for Stevens, "objects act as matrices. . . through which integrations come," she then proceeds to categorically discard or deny the presence of a transcendental impulse in such `integrations,' insisting that Stevens, like the true and pure poet that he was, "fought off persistent tendencies to the transcendent."[82] It seems that in her need to defend Stevens as a `pure' poet, totally immune of any transcendental longings, she must exclude the possibility that the poetic act can, from a purely aesthetic plane, move on to a transcendent one—in itself a dominant tendency in Western literature, and particularly American poetry, since the Romantics.[83] Stevens voices this impulse to give a transcendental slant to his aesthetic experience of things in a late poem, and in words whose meaning is unambiguously clear:

> *The infinite of the actual perceived,*
> *A freedom revealed, a realization touched,*
> *The real made more acute by an unreal.*
>   (*CP* 451)

What Stevens expresses in this tercet is a "desire set deep in the eyes,/Behind all actual seeing" (*CP* 467); that is to say, a `desire' that craves more than the purely aesthetic possession of things, which in Stevens' is the everpresent urge to always try and "make of the poem a miniature eternity."[84] As Marcel Raymond conclusively puts it, "Far from being a rational song, the [modern] poem, extracted from life, always ambiguous like life, represents a kind of supernature," a journey towards "the luminous center of consciousness."[85]

What is finally celebrated in *Harmonium* are not the small, insignificant things of everyday life, but the rebirth of the Stevensian perspectivist and a new poetic idiom following such a rebirth; a new vision of self and world born of the perspectivist's ingrained native pragmatism and passionately affirmative response to the momentous Emersonian question: "Why should we not also enjoy an original relation to the universe?"[86] In commiting himself to this new and `original' relation with the universe, and by an act of immense imaginative reach, the perspectivist is able to convert his hitherto alienated vision of human existence as "a dark and wasteful Chaos" of mere fragments and `multiple truths,' into "a blooming, fertile, heaven-encompassed World."[87] In other words, through an Emersonian `inner leap' or edenic envisioning of reality, the reborn perspectivist manages to transform the brute and impenetrable immanence of the physical universe into something that is "glorious with form, color, and motion";[88] which is to say that he miraculously succeeds by this inner leap to turn what were once the chaotic randomness and irrational disorder of things into the life-giving "fortuities of earth that solace us and make a world."[89] And it is this freshly reborn world now bathed in a new light, in the rediscovered `dizzle-dazzle' of its pristine and intoxicating sensuousness, immanent vigor, color, and sheer physical energy, that sums up one of the poetic glories and dominant themes of *Harmonium*, what Hillis Miller calls "the miraculous recovery of the vitality of earth."[90] And this `recovery of earth,' is affirmed and celebrated, however fleetingly, in "Sunday Morning," one of the most characteristic and memorable pieces in *Harmonium*, where Stevens projects a pagan vision of life along with all the spiritual promises and cures that such a vision holds.[91]

However, the true meaning of this miraculous recovery of earthly delights, born of the passionate union of mind and reality through the intermediacy of the imagination, is the creative impact that such a union has on the perspectivist as an emerging poet; an impact of such magnitude that, for a moment, the radiant, savage beauty of this newly born world and the exultant, imaginative response it sets off in his mind, become one:

> *As the immense dew of Florida*
> *Brings forth*
> *The big-finned palm*
> *And green vine angering for life,*
>
> *As the immense dew of Florida*
> *Brings forth hymn and hymn*
> *From the beholder,*
> *Beholding all these green sides,*
>
> *And blessed mornings,*
> *Meet for the eye of the young alligator,*
> *And lightning colors*
> *So, in me, come flinging*
> *Forms, flames, and the flakes of flames.*
>   (CP 95)

In this magnificent short lyric appropriately entitled "Nomad Exquisite"—Bloom calls it "superbly exuberant"[92]—its twin theme is stated with such force, subtlety, and poetic nuance that we are never quite sure what it is that the poem really celebrates: the birth of a new and vibrant poetic voice or the fierce, untamed grandeur and strength of the physical world—the `immense dew,' `green vine angering for life,' and `blessed mornings'.

However, it is in "Tea at the Palaz of Hoon," a companion piece to "Nomad Exquisite" and according to Bloom a poem equal to "The Snow Man,"[93] that we are given a full portrait of the Stevensian perspectivist as a fully-born poet: an unmistakably Whitmanesque figure who, under an assumed exotic name, poses as a joyously self-assertive celebrant of his burgeoning poetic powers and mind:

> *Not less because in purple I descended*
> *The western day through what you called*
> *The loneliest air, not less was I myself.*
>
> *What was the ointment sprinkled on my beard?*
> *What were the hymns that buzzed beside my ears?*
> *What was the sea whose tide swept through me there?*
>
> *Out of my mind the golden ointment rained,*
> *And my ears made the blowing hymns they heard.*
> *I was myself the compass of that sea:*
>
> *I was the world in which I walked, and what I saw*
> *Or heard or felt came not but from myself;*
> *And there I found myself more truly and more strange.*
>
> (CP 65)

To sum up, what these two early poems in *Harmonium* clearly enunciate in embryonic form and with great power and resonance, are the two central themes that were to dominate and sustain Stevens' poetic canon in the years to come; firstly, the marriage of mind and reality and their endless epistemological war[94]—a war that takes on an almost epic dimension in "An Ordinary Evening in New Haven"; and secondly, the poet's celebration of imagination, not only as life's supreme value and spiritual cure, but also as the indispensable intermediary in this war between mind and reality.[95] As for Stevens' celebration of the imagination as man's highest value, it is expressed with an immense depth of feeling and reverence in "Another Weeping Woman":

> *The magnificent cause of being,*

A Cure of the Mind

The imagination, the one reality
In this imagined world. (CP 25)

Finally, what remains to be clarified are the true poetic characteristics and origin of the Stevensian perspectivist-turned-poet under the assumed persona of Hoon.[96] Richard Poirier, in his recent study of the philosophical roots of modern American poetry (which includes Frost, Stevens, and Stein among others), examines what he calls "the Emersonian pragmatist,"[97] which is his own version of what he considers to be the truly authentic or native American poetic self. According to him, it is a self whose salient characteristic is a blend of Emerson's subversive individualism and William James' rigorous pragmatism. So constituted, the Emersonian pragmatist rejects all received `truths' and perceptions of self and world as being—in James' words—"peptonized and faked," which means that he identifies his dynamic and ever-evolving poetic self with the empiricists' "processive" and "fluxional" physical universe."[98] And this identification springs from the Emersonian pragmatist's fervent belief that what truly obtains is the living moment, and that therefore all `truths' must eventually be bent to his pragmatic will, so that they become " 'versions of the here and the now and [so] flow freely' "; because if there is indeed one thing that the Emersonian poetic self passionately believes in is "that the soul *becomes*" (Emerson), and that in the course of becoming it "engenders [its] truths upon" the world (James).[99] Finally, Poirier identifies Emerson's essay "Circles"—which he uses as primary source for substantiating his argument—as a unique text in that, according to him, it not only best exemplifies Emerson's radical mind and `perceptual transva- luations,'[100] but in so doing, it also increases our understanding of the true origin and nature of the modern American poet as an Emersonian pragmatist.[101]

A Cure of the Mind

As Stevens' most important early persona, sharply conceived and radiantly projected in *Harmonium* where he occupies conspicuously its center-stage, Hoon may be said to possess all the vital characteristics of the Emersonian pragmatist as discussed so far. For one thing, immersed in the creative effulgence of his sudden resurgence as a new and vital poetic self, he identifies his own fermenting `dizzle-dazzle' with the `fluxional' processes and energies of the endlessly burgeoning physical universe; for another, he joyously bears witness and celebrates the fact that "We are not fixed upon any Reality that is beyond or behind or in any way apart,"[102] and therefore, according to him, we live in "an always incipient cosmos," in the world of a moment" "Beyond any order" (*OP* 38,39,15)—words which have the unmistakable stamp and ring of Emerson's own radical `transvaluations.' What is more, as a perpetually evolving and open-ended poetic self, "the creator of an individual mind who becomes his own world"[103]—according to Emerson, a `soul' which *becomes*—Hoon also discovers, in the empiricists' vitally chaotic universe, the very model for his own poetic mind and sensibility. It is a momentous discovery in that, as a practising poet intent on `engendering' his own `truths' upon the world, he feels free to put all inherited ideas to his own use by "troping or inflecting or giving a new voice" to them; that is, he can abandon with impunity "one [poetic] form for the always beckoning promise of another."[104] And this radically innovative approach to poetic creation, this side of solipcism, truly defines the Emersonian pragmatist in Hoon as poet. Moreover, as Poirier points out, it is an approach that has a saving grace; it is a way of writing poetry that it not only helps to generate "the disruptive energies at work" in the poet's subconscious mind, but in so doing it delineates the particular power and appeal of his new poetic—a poetic that both undergirds and sustains *Harmonium* as a whole.[105]

A Cure of the Mind

In his authoritative survey of critical opinion pertaining to *Harmonium* since its appearance in 1923,[106] John Newcomb analyses at great length the inability of Stevens' early commentators—among them sophisticated and seasoned critics like Paul Rosenberg and Louis Untermeyer—to come to grips with the book's baffling obscurities. According to Newcomb, critically open-minded as these critics were in their reading and appreciation of modern poetry, including the new experimental verse that was being written at the time, they were nevertheless incapable of accommodating *Harmonium*'s mixed tonal effects and strange inner music—nonsensical, formal, absurdist, pensive, grandiose, droll, elegiac—as well as its overblown verbal rhetoric and total absence of rational or paraphrasable meaning in most of the poems. However, what really tried the patience of these critics were the titles of the poems in *Harmonium*; not only the fact that a great many of them were outright bizarre, but also the obvious subversive ruse used in doing away, in all cases, with all logical connection whatsoever between a poem's ostensible subject and the title attached to it.[107] Thus, according to Newcomb, such stylistic disjunctions not only "travestied the whole notion of a conventional poetic form," but also subverted the critics' expectations of a unified and consistent vision of self and world, conceived and enunciated in clear aesthetic terms.

As Paul Rosenberg said in summing up his experience in reading *Harmonium*, it was like "The playing of a Chinese orchestra. . .The most amazing cacophony and dissolving labials and silkiest sibilants. . .The falsetto of an ecstatic eunuch."[108]

Thus, according to Newcomb, what actually held back these critics from appreciating the true virtues of *Harmonium*—beyond and above their objections to its stylistic excesses—was the fact that they felt the book represented a new "genetic creation," that is, a new type of verse that had "no prior frame of reference" and had therefore been "purposely" invented by its author in order "*to invoke and enjoy the chaos of the universe*" (emphasis mine).[109] What validates Newcomb's theory as to the failure of Stevens' early critics to come to terms with his first book of poems, is their positive reaction to Eliot's "The Waste Land" published the previous year. Despite the poem's intricate montage, fragmented time sequences, recondite imagery, and thick overlay of obscure literary allusions, the voice that finally does emerge in the poem—regardless how bleak and pessimistic it may have sounded to the ears of these critics—it is a voice of profound inner poise and tonal consistency which, if anything, it enunciates a distinct and coherent vision of modern life by means of a tightly controlled poetic idiom. On the other hand, what these same critics heard in *Harmonium* was a babel of harshly discordant voices that cancelled each other out at every turn, an effect that seemed to betray a mind totally lacking in poetic seriousness and whose aesthetic irreverence, by seeking to deprive poetry of its true `complexity' and `depth,' turned it into an apotheosis of chaos.[110]

But where Stevens' early critics failed most in their reading of *Harmonium*—and which was not the case with their critical appreciation and interpretation of "The Waste Land"—was in their inability to take the full measure of Stevens' own revolutionary verse whose principal aim, according to its author, was to help him express his own "sense of the world," something he could do only by trying "to perceive the normal in the abnormal, the opposite of chaos in chaos" (*NA* 120,153).[111] It is possible that what these critics saw in Stevens' radical poetic in *Harmonium*—his urge `to perceive the normal in the abnormal'—was an offsoot of the new Dadaist-Surrealist aesthetic, which had been founded principally on the imitative fallacy of countering chaos with chaos. On the other hand, the primary aim of Stevens' new poetic was to flesh out, as faithfully as possible, his own apperception of the tensions and modalities of self and world as he himself had experienced them in the first two decades of the twentieth century. It seems, then, that what had made Stevens' early critics incapable of grappling squarely with *Harmonium* were its inherent complexities, which to them appeared both gratuitously subversive and totally incomrehensible.

As Newcomb shrewdly points out in comparing the hermeticism of "The Waste Land" to that of *Harmonium*, all that was required of a sophisticated and learned critic in order to have access to the essential meaning of Eliot's poem was a thorough scholarly gloss of "its allusive textures," that is, the ability to identify and contexualize Eliot's intricate grid of allusions to Shakespeare, Dante, Marvell, Baudelaire, Verlaine, and a number of Eastern sacred texts; on the other hand, however, the hermeticism or ambiguities of *Harmonium* were far more complex in that every single poem in the volume seemed *"to assert the resistance of the poetic subject against all linguistic or conceptual systems that would attempt to circumscribe it"* (emphasis mine).[112] What Newcomb is pointing out here is the failure of Stevens' critics in the 1920s to see him as something more than "a charming decorative artist"[113] or poet-aesthete, who despite the modernist veneer of his verse had obviously not outgrown his 1890s poetic roots. But their yet greatest failure was their critical inability to detect in *Harmonium* the presence of an authentic new poetic language whose primary aim, regardless of its verbal mannerisms and perplexing ambiguities—what Newcomb refers to as Stevens' "alienating strategies"[114]—was to promote Stevens' own version of poetic modernism, namely: `the resistance of the poetic subject against all linguistic or conceptual systems' of interpretation. And this is exactly what distinguishes and defines Stevens' own brand of the modernist poetic venture, and therefore makes it imperative for us to understand the *how* and the *why*, the nature and purpose of his complexity and ambiguity, his persistence in making poetic speech as difficult as possible for the reader through `the resistance of the poetic subject.'

In most cases, Stevens' inaccessible meanings and overall obscurity derive mainly from the ambiguousness of his tropes and figurative language in general; therefore, in knowing the way his tropes are born and then made to conceal the subject of a poem, we can come to understand the inner workings of his creative mind and as a result have better access to the intended meanings of his poems. Drawn from the deepest layers of his subconscious, and given the full play and range of his imagination, Stevens' perceptions do not seem to go through any check points set up by the rational mind, so that they carry the same meaning they had been given at the time of their inception. Irvin Ehrenpreis gives an accurate and lucid description of this aspect of the creative process in Stevens:

> *The inmost self is subrational and prelinguistic. It holds the feelings and tastes that move us to speech, not those that issue from speech. Stevens' [perceptions] bypass the conscious, literary, reflective mind, as music does, to suggest the impulses that determine poetry from within and that link it to the reality enveloping and dominating us from without.*[115]

Thus, paradoxically, by avoiding miraculously the fatal pitfalls of solipsism, and so entrenching their strong imaginative hold on us, Stevens' seemingly intractable tropes, in seeking to impede our understanding of his poetic subjects, eventualy augment their spell and attraction over us, since they make us stay with them in our stubborn efforts to extract from them their intended meaning and imaginative logic.[116] And in the course of our concerted efforts to find out what their ultimate meaning is, we finally discover that Stevens' tropes have "a value *separate from their meaning in terms of human speech*"; that is to say, they have "a

31

sense value different from, if not *entirely independent* of, their meaning to the literate mind."[117]

For example, in "The Emperor of Ice-Cream," Stevens' powerful invocation of modern death and a poetic text distinguished for its paradigmatic ambiguous tropes, the title of the poem could be easily said to allude to either life or death, or both;[118] likewise, drawn as a comically ominous film-noir mobster, "the roller of big cigars" could conceivably be troped into a parish priest ("the muscular one"), asked to attend the wake of a dead madam in a 1920s speakeasy. Despite the poem's perplexing ambiguousness, if given the close reading it surely deserves, its obscure tropes can be made to yield a clarity all their own, eventually amplified for us by Stevens' pivotal quasi-philosophical exhortation delivered halfway in the poem: "Let be be the finale of seem." The exhortation is voiced with such urgent conviction as to make its meaning unequivocally clear: the physical universe or the world at large is devoid of spiritual content or a higher realm of being wherein we can escape and transcend our human condition; consequently, we can look upon the appearance of things and the essence we choose to attach to them as coterminous, since all reality—ontological, noumenal, transcendental—is ultimately subsumed in the empirical. Thus, in bringing this philosophical insight to bear on his vision of modern death, Stevens makes such a vision clearer for us by focusing our attention on those grimly empirical details that best underscore the woman's alienated and desacralized death: her "cold," "dumb" face and protruding "horny feet," as well as the flowers brought by `the boys' wrapped "in last month's newspapers." As for the diffuse sexual atmosphere pervading the entire scene—the "wenches'" manner of dress as they "dawdle" about the room, and the "concupiscent curds" being whipped in the kitchen—it helps to further enhance the squalid face of modern death as projected in the poem. As a result, sex and death, two of man's most primal experiences, are brought together and made to share the horrendous facticity and alienation to which they have been reduced in the modern world. Whatever glimmer of hope or salvation is to be found in such a world, this can only be a matter of personal choice or inner vision; which is what Stevens insinuates in what I consider to be one of the truly germane tropes in the poem: "Let the lamp affix its beam."

Discarding for the present the issue of solopsism, the extent to which Stevens' ambiguities tend to elude `the literate mind' by challenging "the reader's conventional dualisms of form and meaning,"[119] the fact remains that "The Emperor of Ice-Cream," as a finished poetic artifact, supercedes all its purported difficulties. Its greatness lies in its internal unity, in the way Stevens has devised and framed its imagery, tropes, diction, and formal structure in order to flesh out, in the most concrete, imaginative terms possible, his intense and clear vision of life and death in the modern world. This still leaves unanswered, however, the teasing absurdity of the poem's title: why `emperor, and particularly one given to trafficking in ice-cream? Needless to say, such a question lies outside the compass of our critical capacity or clairvoyance, since it can only precipitate endless exegetical second-guessing and critical theorizing; therefore, given Stevens' own belief in `the irrational element' of poetic creation, the fact that for him "There is a point at which the intelligence destroys poetry" (*L* 305), we have no choice but to accept the puzzling obscurity of his titles at their face value, that is, as part of his conception of poetry and therefore as being beyond the ken of rational apprehension or interpretation. We can, however, have an idea as to how Stevens' titles are conceived and made to work against the poetic subjects whose meanings they are supposed to undergird and amplify for us. Verbal mutations born in the heat of intense poetic emotion,

Stevens' seemingly alogical phrases, tropes, and wayward titles have their source in what Ehrenpreis calls our "archetypal memory" or "premordial response to the world" where, given the freest possible imaginative play and strongest metaphoric impress, they are made to "convey precise suggestions of attitudes or feelings" which, on account of their semantic opacity, remain outside the framework of our conventional modes of linguistic decoding—in short, beyond the grasp of "myth, symbolism, [and] human association."[120]

In summing up this discussion of Stevens' ambiguous tropes and overall obscurity with reference to the poems in *Harmonium*, there are two crucial and closely related points that need to be stressed; crucial in the sense that they go a long way in helping us understand the complex workings of Stevens' poetic mind, and also in validating one of my central arguments in this essay. The two points are as follows: firstly, Stevens' intractable but alluring tropes, dredged up as they are from the deepest pools of subconscious thought and feeling, not only give ample evidence of the perspectivist's inner drama of floundering perpetually in "the torments of confusion" (*CP* 27), but also show the extent to which the perspectivist uses poetic troping as a means of assuaging such `torments,' that is, his oppressive sense of inner and outer chaos; and secondly, Stevens' tropes betray an impelling urge to always want to express even his most mundane impressions, thoughts, and feelings in verbally elaborate and complex figurations; in fact to such an extreme degree that one finally begins to suspect that this is not the case of a poetic sensibility passionately engaged in fulfilling the exacting requirements of an aesthetic ideal (Flaubert, Mallarmé, Joyce), but of a pressing inner need that lies outside the compass of poetic creation and is deeply rooted in the perspectivist's own fragmented phenomenology.

A Cure of the Mind

As a `connoisseur of chaos,' living in a `world of chaotic mutation'[121] and stripped of all metaphysical, religious, and aesthetic props, the perspectivist poet knows only too well that "the creation of poetry. . .can begin only at the point where the world becomes unintelligible."[122] Thus his "tough, diverse, aesthetic" (*CP* 31) and closely affined strategies—his poetic disjunctions and bizarre personas: "Socrates of snails," "lutanist of fleas," weeping burgher," "nomad exquisite," or self-celebrant Hoon—become his revenge against the chaotic world he lives in, as well as his most effective means of distancing and protecting himself from it. Finally, as a radically new and finely tuned linguistic medium, the perspectivist's `tough' verse is assigned two specific tasks: (a) to register with the highest possible verbal precision his ceaseless valuations of self and world; and (b) by drawing heavily upon the metaphoric resources of language, to provide a cure[123] for the feverish searchings and inner convolutions of his fragmented consciousness. For example, Crispin's *logodaedalian*[124] mind, given to its manic quest for a new aesthetic as well as endless speculations concerning the penetralium of things—though always aware of the fact that the mind is "nibbling at the sugared void" (*CP* 43)—seems to have found in its profuse, dizzying tropes and violent verbal disjunctions, a new ground for self-renewal or remedy for its deeply disoriented phenomenology of self and world. And it is exactly at this point, the extreme degree to which the perspectivist resorts to disjunctive troping in order to express and also alleviate his awareness of a chaotic world—including his own self—that he undertakes to violate all notions of rationality and, by so doing, turn his `tough' and `diverse' poetic into "an obscuring rather than a clarifying medium."[125]

The perspectivist's dire—we might even say tragic—predicament then, is the fact that each time he emerges from one of his tortuous descents into poetic creation or "dance of tropes,"[126] he invariably finds himself mired in self-despair; a despair that stems from the painful realization that what all his impassioned forays into poetic irrationality—his exotic personas, bizarre titles, or baffling tropes—finally amount to is "a lustred nothingness" (*CP* 320): the fact that all his brilliantly conceived poetic figurations and involuted meanings prove to be totally unreal and therefore only useful in "making visible/The motions of the mind (and) giving form/To moodiest nothings" (*CP* 137). Thus what is eventually salvaged out of the perspectivist's shattering disillusion is a quasi-philosophical precept, which he announces to us in a tone of exultant despair:

> *It is a world of words to the end of it,*
> *In which nothing solid is its solid self.* (*CP* 345)

It is this highly fluid and centerless conception of art, self, and world that in the end impels the perspectivist to turn the creative act into a `cure of the mind'; as a result, we have no choice but to accept all his poetic acts as semi-solipsistic self-creations,[127] whose ultimate meaning and human appeal must remain self-sealed to the end. In conclusion, we can say that the perspectivist's success as a poet is predicated on this challenging and telling paradox: living in a world where `nothing solid is its solid self,' and therefore having to sustain such a precariously unstable vision of life by dint of his own profusely perspectivizing imagination, he must somehow manage to keep the solipsist in him at bay but also within reach; in other words, he must know *when* and *how* to let his wayward mind swing, freely and creatively, between the strong pull of his inner urges and the rigorous requirements of his art. And it is the extent to which he firmly disciplines this freedom that the Stevensian perspectivist may be said to achieve his distinctive power and appeal as a poet.

A Cure of the Mind

NOTES

1. In his *A Homemade World: The American Modernist Writers* (New York: Knopf, 1975), pp.53,69,70, Hugh Kenner, in rejecting outright Stevens' poetry, refers to his style as "a kind of bankruptcy" and "a noble imposture," whose "rhetorical convolutions move uncomfrortably close to the ridiculous." On a milder note, P.R. Blackmur observes that "Stevens' obscuracies" are due to "the essential impenetrability of words," while Randall Jarrell berates the American poet for his stylistic excesses, which make his longer poems sound like "quasi-philosophical day dreams"; and finally, for Irving Howe and Donald Davie, Stevens is "a gaudy mystifier" whose language often degenerates into "a sort of vulgar splendour." However, on the other hand, Bernard Bengonzi has the greatest admiration for Stevens' poetry, in particular for "Its ingenuity and wit and colourfulness," and considers him "a superb styl[ist]," with "the purest diction of any living poet." For sources of citations, see *Stevens: The Critical Heritage*, ed. Doyle, pp.115, 333, 385-90, 428, 437.

2. J. Hillis Miller, "Stevens' `Rock' and Criticism as Cure," in *Modern Critical Views*, ed. Bloom, p.34.

3. According to Miller, such complexity brings Stevens' verse "below the level of rational thinking" (*The Linguistic Moment*, p.13).

4. Miller, *Poets of Reality*, p.259. There may not be "a theory of life" in Stevens but he has a strong, pervasive vision of it which he inherited in part from the American empiricists. For them, the physical universe is a conglomeration of chaotically random, empirical particulars without a center, design, or purpose. Similarly, in his darkest, most reductive moments Stevens envisions the world as "a moving chaos that never ends" (*OP* 50), a vision that also informs his conception of human consciousness and mind: "The mind's own limits, like a tragic thing/Without existence, existing everywhere," "Like the wind that lashes everything at once" (*CP* 298,358). For William James' influence on Stevens' thought and poetry, see David M. Laguardia, *Advance*

on Chaos: The Sanctifying Imagination of Wallace Stevens (Hanover, Pa.: The University Press of New England, 1983), pp.1-35; Stanley J. Scott, "Wallace Stevens and Williams James: The Poetics of Pure Experience," *Philosophy and Literature* 1 (1977): 183-91, and Ihab Hassan, "Imagination and Belief: Wallace Stevens and Williams James," *The Wallace Stevens Journal* 10 (1981): 3-8.

5.   Miller, "Theoretical and Atheoretical in Stevens," p.282.

6.   The sense in which I am using these labels, `discontinuities' or `principle of discontinuity,' goes beyond the obvious disjunctions of thought and structure, what Miller calls Stevens' `breaks into the formal order of thought and shapely poetry.' By `discontinuities' I am specifically referring to the intrinsic and gratuitous obscurity of Stevens' poetic tropes which, as such, exist in a self-sealed verbal vacuum all of their own. Such tropes, present in most of the longer poems, are particularly dominant in "Like Decorations in a Nigger Cemetery," "Variations on a Summer Day," "Montrachet-le-Jardin," "Chocorua to Its Neighbor," "Description without Place," "The Auroras of Autumn," "The Owl in the Sarcophagus," "Someone Puts a Pineapple Together," and in most of the cantos in "An Ordinary Evening in New Haven."

7.   For a historical overview of the major theoritical approaches to Stevens' poetry with in-depth commentaries, see Melita Schaum, *Wallace Stevens' and the Critical Schools* (Tuscaloosa: University of Alabama Press, 1988), and John T. Newcomb, *Wallace Stevens and Literary Canons* (Jackson, Miss.: University Press of Mississippi, 1992).

8.   Stevens' major ideas, used in different contexts in his poetry, are `chaos,' `center,' `nothing'/'nothingness,' `the first idea,' `decreation,' and `fictions.' For the best critical discussion of `decreation' and `fictions,' see Roy Harvey Pearce, "Toward Decreation: Stevens and the Theory of Poetry," in *A Celebration*, ed. Doggett and Buttel, pp.286-307; Frank Kermode, *The Sense of*

an Ending: Studies in the Theory of Fiction (New York: Oxford University Press, 1967), pp.35-64; and Frank Lentricchia, *After the New Criticism*, pp.28-60. Also, for a detailed discussion of Stevens' major ideas in general, see B. J. Leggett, *Wallace Stevens and Poetic Theory; passim.*

9. A case in point is Roy Harvey Pearce's approach to Stevens, who, in his otherwise monumental work, *The Continuity of American Poetry* (Princeton University Press, 1963), would have us believe that Stevens is an Adamic humanist in the great American literary tradition.

10. See Stevens' essay, "The Irrational Element in Poetry" (*OP* 216-29), where he defends the use of the irrational in poetry.

11. For consultation concerning Stevens' wide-ranging readings in poetic theory, philosophy, and related subjects, see his *Commonplace Book* (*SCB*), particularly pp.113-17.

12. "Poet of Mind and Reality," an unsigned review in Doyle, *The Critical Heritage*, p.459.

13. As Frank Doggett points out in *Stevens' Poetry of Thought* (Baltimore, Md.: Johns Hopkins Press, 1966), p.109: "the poet in him [Stevens] always subordinates idea to the uses of poetry." Concerning Stevens' vacillating poetic mind, Charles Olson's personal testimony is both revealing and instructive: "He spoke in sentences, not in paragraphs. There was no such thing as a connected argument. What you had instead was a series of intuitive and highly perceptive remarks. When he got on a subject, he would talk with flashes of intuition. That was not a man who thought consecutively." This is definitely the kind of mind heard speaking in Stevens' longer poems. See Peter Brazeau, *Parts of a World: Wallace Stevens Remembered* (New York: Random House, 1983), p.211.

14. In Stevens the boundaries of philosophical thought and poetic perception are often blurred, so that for him access to "the veritable ding an sich" (*CP* 29) of reality is open to both

philosophy and poetry. As he says in one of his poems: "To get at the thing/Without gestures is to get at it as/Idea" (*CP* 295). For further glosses on this theme, see also *CP* 183, 373, 471.

15. In one of his lesser poems entitled "The Role of the Idea in Poetry" (*OP* 93), Stevens tells the reader to "Ask the philosopher why he philosophizes," the answer being, as implied in the poem as a whole, that the primary aim of philosophy is integration. Sanford Scwartz, in his discussion of Nietzsche, Bergson, James, and Bradley, points out that "According to James, poetic creation and philosophical conception `have the same function'"; and he goes on to quote James to the effect that "The poet's words and the philosopher's phrases thus are helps of the most genuine sort, giving to all of us hereafter the freedom of the trails they made." See *The Matrix of Modernism: Pound, Eliot, and Early 20th-Century Thought* (Princeton, N. J.: Princeton University Press, 1985, p.48.

16. At such reductive, apocalyptic moments, Stevens looks upon all human culture as a vast repository of dead ideas and myths, so that to him "The integrations of the past are like/A *Museo Olympico*, so little, our affair" (*CP* 342), and in his poetry he refers to all past conceptualizations of self and world as "rotted names" (*CP* 183), garbage-dump (*CP* 201), and "junk-shop" (*CP* 218).

17. Says Stevens: "My reality-imagination complex is entirely my own even though I see it in others" (*L* 792); however, he hastens to add that "The constant discussion of imagination and reality is largerly a discussion not for the purposes of life but for the purposes of arts and letters" (*NA* 147). As a critical formula, the imagination-reality conflict has been the mainstay and principal matrix in all major studies of Stevens to date, mainly because—one is tempted to suspect—it allows for almost unlimited critical speculation and theorization, while at the same time it manages to conveniently mute the crucial question as to the true provenance and nature of Stevens' `irrational' and `savage' poetic voice.

18. Miller, *Poets of Reality*, p.258.

19. Ibid., p.225. Miller also believes Stevens to be "one of the subtlest expositors of the tradition" (perspectivism), and cites Feuerbach, Dilthey, Nietzsche, Ortega y Gasset, Santayana, and Henri Focillon as "his predecessors" (p.224). My own thesis, central to this essay, is that Stevens' poetic `perspectives' are pure self-creations, fulfilling some urgent, ontological inner need, and as such have very little connection with empirical reality. For this reason, and the lack of a better term, I like to refer to this aspect of Stevens' mind as *mental perspectivism*. With regard to the term `perspectivist' as I am using the term in this essay, it refers in general to modern man; a being who, having lost all his inner props (metaphysical, religious, aesthetic) that make for a stable and structured self, lives in a world totally devoid of "*eternal horizons or perspectives.*" In a stricter sense, the label `perspectivist poet' is used as a figuration to describe Stevens' overall poetic persona as projected in his mind and poetry. As such, he may be said to be "a disoriented voyager without a heaven" or `center'; a poet whose fragmented mind is caught in an endless cycle of "perceptual transvaluations" and disjunctive tropes—all part and parcel of a complex poetic sensibility seeking to create for itself an ideal but viable new self. For sources of citations, see Fernando Molina, *Existentialism as Philosophy* (Englewood Cliffs, N.J.: Prentice-Hall, 1962), p.23, and M.H. Abrams, *Natural Supernaturalism: Tradition and Revolution in Romantic Literature* (New York: Norton, 1973), pp.312,539.

20. The texts that have helped me most in formulating my argument about Stevens' own perspectivism, are the following: Henri Bergson, "Introduction to Metaphysics," *The Search for Being: Essays from Kierkegaard to Sartre on the Problem of Existence*, ed. Jean T. Widle and William Kimmel (New York: Noonday Press, 1962) pp.175-204; the chapters "Doctrine of the Point of View" and "The Significance of the Theory of Einstein," José Ortega y Gasset, *The Modern Theme*, trans. James Cleugh (New York: Harper Torchbooks, 1961), pp.86-96,135-52; the chapter "Perspectivism," Arthur C. Danto, *Nietzsche as Philosopher* (New York: Macmillan, 1965), pp.68-99; James McFarlane, "The Mind

41

of Modernism," in *Modernism: 1890-1930*, ed. Bradbury and McFarlane, pp.71-93; the section "Perspectivism and Relativity," Ricardo C. Quinones, *Mapping Literary Modernism: Time and Development* (Princeton, N. J.: Princeton University Press, 1985), pp.114-19; and the chapter "Cinders: A Sketch of a New Weltanschauung," T.E. Hulme, *Speculations: Essays on Humanism and the Philosophy or Art*, ed. Herbert Read (New York, Harcourt, Brace, 1924), pp.215-45.

21. Quoted in Danto, *Nietzsche*, p.32. Cf. Hulme's statement: "There is no such thing as an absolute truth to be discovered. All general statements about truth, etc., are in the end only amplifications of man's appetites" (*Speculations*, p.217).

22. Ibid.

23. Lentricchia, *After the New Criticism*, p.236. Modern perspectivism, in general, has its beginnings in Emerson: "There are no fixtures in nature. The universe is fluid and volatile." Quoted in Harold Bloom, *Wallace Stevens: The Poems of Our Climate* (Ithaca and London: Cornell University Press, 1976), p.310.

24. Schwartz, *Matrix of Modernism*, p.224.

25. Nietzsche quoted in James Collins, *The Existentialists: A Critical Study* (Chicago: Gateway Books, 1964), pp.49-50. It is interesting to note that Jacqueline Vaught Brogan identifies deconstruction as "A radical post-Nietzschean perspectivism that unmasks the imaginary stability of solid concepts and other metaphysical and ideological universals." See *Stevens and Simile: A Theory of Language* (Princeton, N.J.: Princeton University Press, 1986), p.233.

26. The phrase is Nietzsche's, quoted in Schwartz, *Matrix of Modernism*, p.5. Schwartz goes on to point out that Barthes' idea of the `absolutely plural text' "is derived from Nietzsche's vision of reality as a sensory flux irreducible to determinate order" (Ibid., p.224). Cf.Hulme's statement: "All is flux. The moralists, the capital letterists, attempt to find a framework outside the flux, a

solid bank for the river, a pier rather than a raft" (*Speculations*, p.222).

27. McFarlane, "The Mind of Modernism," p.83. See also Ortega's ironic rejection of abstract philosophical systems: "Their clear and simple schematic pattern, their ingenuous illusion of being discoveries of truth in its entirety. . .convey the impression of a closed circle, defined and definitive, where there are no more problems to solve and everything is satisfactorily determined" (*Modern Theme*, p.94).

28. Quinones, *Mapping Literary Modernism*, pp.115,117.

29. Ibid., p.115.

30. *The Portable Emerson*, ed. Carl Bode and Malcolm Cowley (Harmondsworth, Middlesex, Penguin, 1983), p.228. In seeking to make a connection between the physicists' relativist theories and literary modernism, Quinones maintains that "the strength of Modernism [is] its ability to present a rich variety of perspectives, all of which are `true'" (Ibid., p.117). However, in making this connection he leaves out Emerson, whose three essays "Nature," "Circles," and "Experience" I consider to be primary sources for modernist perspectivism in general; as Alfred Kazin points out, for Emerson "God had become a matter of pieces, fragments, glowing moments." See *An American Procession* (London: Seeker and Warburg, 1985), p.62.

31. McFarlane, "The Mind of Modernism," p.83.

32. Cf. Pound's description of Mauberley's consciousness as "disjunct"; *Selected Poems* (London: Faber and Faber, 1981), p.111.

33. As a dominant persona, the poet-perspectivist appears in Stevens' poetry under various disguises; see in particular, "Domination of Black" (*CP* 8), "The Doctor of Geneva" (*CP* 24), "The Comedian as the Letter C" (*CP* 27), "From the Misery of Don Joost" (*CP* 46), "Anecdote of the Prince of Peacocks" (*CP* 57), "The Weeping Burgher" (*CP* 61), "Girl in a Nightgown" (*CP* 214), "Connoisseur

of Chaos" (*CP* 215), and "The Well Dressed Man with a Beard" (*CP* 247).

34. Molina, *Existentialism as Philosophy*, p.24.

35. Wylie Sypher, *Loss of the Self in Modern Literature* (New York: Vintage Books, 1964), p.96.

36. See my discussion of `bareness' as a figuration for modern man's spiritual impoverishment and isolation, in *Crispin's Voyage: The Search for a Vital Center in the Poetry of Wallace Stevens* (Athens: 1991), pp.43-45.

37. Cf. the lines in "The Wind Shifts": "The wind shifts like this:/Like a human without illusions" (*CP* 83). As Roland Sukenick points out in his reading of the poem: "We read into reality our own human feelings"; *Wallace Stevens: Musing the Obscure* (New York: New York University Press, 1967), p.231.

38. My main concern here is with Crispin the perspectivist poet-in-the-making and not with the quester for a `vital center,' as was the case with my discussion of Crispin in my previous monograph. Ultimately, the final resolution to all of Crispin's endless epistemological speculations, his `visions and revisions,' remains aesthetic. As A. Walton Litz correctly observes, the essential meaning and outcome of Crispin's inner odyssey can only be described as "an introspective voyage of poetic discovery." See *Introspective Voyager* (New York: Oxford University Press, 1972), p.129.

39. Nathan A. Scott, *The Poetics of Belief: Studies in Coleridge, Arnold, Pater, Santayana, Stevens and Heidegger* (Chapel Hill: The University of North Carolina Press), p.69.

40. Says Stevens: "I do seek a centre and expect to go on seeking it. It is the great necessity even without specific identification." Quoted in Michel Belamou, *Wallace Stevens and the Symbolist Imagination* (Princeton N. J.: Princeton University Press, 1972), p.84. Also, "Artificial Populations" (*OP* 112) begins with the revealing line: "The center that he sought was a state of mind."

41. In his discussion of Georg Simmel's theory of "the aestheticization of reality" as a social phenomenon that lies "at the heart of the modernist experience," David Frisby goes on to say, quoting the German thinker, that due to `"all the oscillations and the fragmentariness of empirical existence. . .this longing to escape from life's complexity and constant unrest. . .assumes an aesthetic character. [People] seem to find in the artistic conception of things a release from the fragmentary and painful in real life."' See *Fragments of Modernity: Theories of Modernity in the Work of Simmel, Kracauer and Benjamin* (Cambridge: Polity Press, 1985), pp.40, 44-45. Simmel's theory provides the essential matrix for the `aestheticization' of Crispin's own life.

42. Inadvertently, "Landscape with Boat" also touches upon the tragic irony of William James' own spiritual plight: the arch-empiricist and tough-minded philosophical pragmatist who, having single-handedly debunked all Idealist metaphysics and claims to a `higher truth' as conceptually fake, subsequently discovers and laments the absence of a cohering `center' in his own life: "I feel that there is a center in truth's forest where I have never been: to track it down and get there is the secret spring of my poor life's philosophic efforts." Quoted in LaGuardia, *Advance on Chaos*, p.27. But even a greater irony, in this respect, is to be found among present-day deconstructionists, for whom the very notion of `center' as an epistemological postulate signifies spiritual death. Says Derrida: "Is not center, the absense of play and difference, another name for death?" See *Writing and Difference*, trans. Alan Bass, (Chicago: Chicago University Press, 1978).

43. The basis of all Stevens' thought and poetry is expressed in an eloquent and moving description of the vanishing of the gods from the consciousness of modern man: "To see the gods dispelled in mid-air and dissolve like clouds is one of the great human experiences. It is not as if they had gone over the horizon to disappear for a time; nor as if they had been overcome by other gods of greater power and profounder knowledge. It is simply that they came to nothing. Since we have always shared all things with

them and have always had a part of their strength and, certainty, all of their knowledge, we shared likewise this experience of annihilation. It was their annihilation, not ours, and yet it left us feeling that in a measure we, too, had been annihilated. It left us feeling dispossessed and alone in a solitude, like children without parents, in a home that seemed deserted, in which the amical rooms and halls had taken on a look of hardness and emptiness. What was most extraordinary is that they left no momentoes behind, no thrones, no mystic rings, no texts either of the soil or of the soul. It was as if they had never inhabited the earth." (*OP* 206-7).

44. J.S. Leonard and C.E. Wharton, *The Fluent Mundo: Wallace Stevens and the Structure of Poetry* (Athens, Georgia: The University of Georgia Press, 1986), p.31.

45. Richard Poirier, *The Renewal of Literature: Emersonian Reflections* (New York: Random House, 1987), p.211.

46. As I point out in *Crispin's Voyage* (p.2), Helen Vendler is the only one among Stevens' major scholars who believes that the poem's subject is serious and skirts the tragic." See *On Extended Wings: Wallace Stevens' Longer Poems* (Cambridge, MA: Harvard University Press, 1969), p.38.

47. It is such lines—'a bright *scienza* beyond ourselves'—which reaffirm my belief that Stevens is at heart a transcendental monist. See also the question posed in "Extracts from Addresses to the Academy of Fine Ideas": "Is it the multitude of thoughts/Like insects in the depths of the mind, that kill/The single thought?" (*CP* 254).

48. Emerson, a true illuminist relying on his `inner light' or epiphanic moments to build for him a durable imaginative world beyond the self, reverses the order: "The reason why the world lacks unity, and lies broken in heaps, is because a man is disunited with himself." He does, however, get on the right track when he wisely says that "Every spirit builds itself a house, and beyond its house a

world, and beyond its world a heaven" (*Portable Emerson*, pp.48,49).

49. I believe that this was Stevens' essential vision of self and world to the end of his life. He was congenitally incapable of creating for himself a personal `mythology' or intimate human world that he could use as a scaffolding for his imagination, as was the ease with Yeats, Eliot, Williams, Frost, Faulkner, and Hemingway.

50. Lentricchia, *After the New Criticism*, p.325.

51. Miller, *Poets of Reality*, p.230

52. Michael H. Levenson, *A Genealogy of Modernism: A Study of English Literary Doctrine 1908-1922* (Cambridge: Cambridge University Press, 1990), p.184.

53. Borrowed from F.H. Bradley's *Appearence and Reality*, the notion of `finite centres' constitutes the basis of Eliot's empiricist poetics and addresses itself to the empirical data of consciousness associated with time, space, duration, causality, and the primary qualities of material objects. A confirmed philosophical empiricist, Bradley was at heart a monist who sought to synthesize and subsume the complex disparities of empirical reality in a higher unity, his so-called Absolute. For a full discussion of Bradley's `finite centres' and the Absolute as related to Eliot's poetics in general, see Levenson (Ibid., pp.176-93), and Schwartz, *Matrix of Modernism*, pp.31-36, 156-62. Also, for a short and lucid account of Bradley's main ideas in *Appearence and Reality*, see John Passmore, *A Hundred Years of Philosophy* (Harmonds- worth, Middlesex: Penguin, 1968), pp.60-71.

54. Due to their abstractness, key terms in the Stevens canon like `truth' and `reality' require some clarification. As variously commented upon by a number of critics over the years, the word `truth,' as used in the famous line "Where was it one first heard of the truth? The the" ("Man on the Dump"), may refer to "the reflective life of the mind as well as the life of the senses"; or, again, it may refer strictly to the self's empirical experiences or

acquired `beliefs' (Bloom, *Wallace Stevens*, p.147). As for the word `reality,' Frank Doggett provides the best interpretation of its multiple meanings found in Stevens' poetry: "*Reality*, in Stevens' use of the word, may be the world supposed to be antecedent in itself or the world created in the specific occurrence of thought, including the thinker himself and his mind forming the thought. Often the term offers the assumption that if the self is the central point of a circle of infinite radius, then *reality* is the not-self, including all except the abstract subjective center. Sometimes *reality* is used in the context of the nominalist position—then the word denotes that which is actual and stands as a phenomenal identity, the existent as opposed to the merely fancied. Stevens usually means by *reality* an undetermined base on which a mind constructs its personal sense of the world. Occasionally he will use the word *real* as a term of approval, as a substitute for the word *true*, and therefore, no more than an expression of confidence" (*Stevens' Poetry of Thought*, p.307).

55. For a full discussion of Romantic poetic doctrine and its relation to modern poetry, see Abrams, *Natural Supernaturalism*, pp.373-99. Also, in *Reflections on the Death of a Porcupine and Other Essays* (Bloomington, Ind.: Indiana University Press, 1963), p.229, D.H. Lawrence underscores, in his own vivid way, the Romantic writers' vital rediscovery of the physical universe: "Voltaire, Shelley, Wordsworth, Byron, Rousseau. . .established a new connection between mankind and the universe, and the result was a vast release of energy. The sun was reborn to man, so was the moon." His phrase, `the *sun* was reborn to man' is crucially central and applicable to both Stevens' metaphysic and aesthetic as projected in his poetry.

56. "Stevens and Williams: The Epistemology of Modernism," in *The Poetics of Modernism*, ed. Gelpi, p.5.

57. Scott, *Poetics of Belief*, p.14.

58. *The Poems of Gerald Manley Hopkins*, ed. W.H. Gardner and N.H. Mackenzie (London: Oxford University Press, 1967), p.66.

59. Scott, *Poetics of Belief*, p.95.

60. Quoted in Abrams, *Natural Supernaturalism*, p.378.

61. Ibid., p.397. The phrase sums up perfectly Abrams' general thesis and provides his monumental study with its grand theme, which he formulates as follows: "The title *Natural Supernaturalism* indicates that my recurrent, but far from exclusive, concern will be with the secularization of inherited theological ideas and ways of thinking. . .Much of what distinguishes writers I call `Romantic' derives from the fact that they undertook. . .to save traditional concepts, schemes, and values which had been based on the relation of the Creator to his creatures and creation [and] reformulate them within the prevailing two-term system of subject and object, ego and non-ego, the human mind or consciousness and its transactions with nature" (p.12-13). Walter Pater, like a true protomodernist, once told a fellow academic: "I think that there is a. . .sort of religious phase possible for the modern mind, the condition of which phase is the main object of my design to convey." Quoted in Graham Hough, *The Last Romantics* (London: Methuen, 1961), p.145. Also, in his novel *Marius the Epicurean* (New York: Modern Library, n.d.), p.274, Pater provides the supreme paradigm of such a phase wherein sensory perception, aesthetic emotion, and religious sentiment are equally present: "the light which creeps at a particular hour on a particular picture or space upon the wall, the scent of flowers in the air at a particular window, become to her, *not so much apprehended objects, as themselves powers of apprehension and doorways to things beyond*" (emphasis mine). It is worth noting how the young Stevens, as a budding and more empirically tempered modernist poet, in a strikingly similar situation disallows any religious feeling from obtruding into what is for him a purely sensuous and aesthetic experience: "In the afternoon I sat in the piano room reading Keats' "Endymion," and listening to the ocassional showers on the foliage outside. . .Once as I looked up I saw a big, pure drop of rain slip from leaf to leaf of a clematis vine. The thought occurred to me that it was just such quick, unexpected, commonplace,

specific things that poets and other observers jot down in their notebooks. It was certainly a monstrous pleasure to be able to be specific about such a thing" (*SP* 45).

62. Ibid., pp.384, 421. It is worth noting how Stevens, as a young Wordsworthian (1902), expresses a similar sentiment using Carlyle's own words: "As I went tramping through the fields and woods, I beheld every leaf and blade of grass revealing or rather betokening the Invisible" (*L* 59).

63. Scott, *Poetics of Belief*, pp.99,133.

64. Frederick. J. Hoffman, *The Mortal No: Death and the Modern Imagination* (Princeton, N. J.: Princeton University Press, 1964), p.349.

65. Erich Heller, *The Disinherited Mind: Essays on Modern German Literature and Thought* (Cambridge: Bowes & Bowes, 1952), p.114. The statement describes Rilke's conception of poetry, what he calls `*herzwerk*,' which addresses the modern poet's supreme challenge to try and create a new sanctity out of a world of pure immanence (pp.126-27).

66. James Joyce, *Ulysses* (New York: Vintage Books, 1961), p.37.

67. Notwithstanding their radical differences in aesthetic creed or poetic practice, all modernist poets have one thing in common: their lost Christian faith and the vestiges of what Geoffrey Hartman refers to as `transcendental feelings.' Thus, even for a tough-minded nominalist like Ezra Pound, one of the primary aims of poetry is to limn the epiphanic particular or `luminous detail' out of the brute anonymity of one's personal life, history, culture, and poetic tradition, so as to make the "world eternally present" (Guy Davenport) and thereby turn the poetic act itself into "a search for eternal, archetypal situations" (Hugh Kenner). For sources of citations, see Marjorie Perloff, *The Dance of the Intellect: Studies in the Poetry of the Pound Tradition* (Cambridge: Cambridge University Press, 1985), pp.10,22. For a discussion of Pound's idea of the `luminous detail' as related to Joyce's

epiphanies, see Herbert N. Schneidau, *Ezra Pound: The Image and the Real* (Baton Rouge: Louisiana State University Press, 1969), pp.74-109.

68. Joyce, by epiphanizing the impenetrable immanence of things, blots out the void looming beyond. As young Daedalus says to a fellow student, the mind "divides the entire universe into two parts, the object, and the void which in not the object." See *Stephen Hero*, ed. Theodore Spencer (New York: New Directions, 1944), p.212.

69. Litz, *Introspective Voyager*, p.iv.

70. Marcel Raymond, *From Baudelaire to Surrealism* (London: Methuen, 1970), p.7.

71. Miller, "William Carlos Williams," *Poets of Reality*, pp.307,313.

72. As John Newcomb observes in *Literary Canons*, p.153: "Bravura, springlike, sensuous, musical, light, these were the virtues of *Harmonium* seized upon and celebrated by postwar critics." Thus the figure that looms in the background of *Harmonium*, as an American progenitor and celebrant of nature's `dizzle-dazzle,' is Emerson. Although a staunch transcendentalist who believes that "visible nature must have a spiritual and moral side," what he truly reveres is the physical world: "nature glorious with form, color, and motion" (*Portable Emerson*, pp.25,28). These also happen to be the supreme qualities of *Harmonium*.

73. Raymond, *From Baudelaire to Surrealism*, p.4.

74. This impassioned belief in the living and inviolable `integrity' of material things (Williams) often betrays—again in Hartman's phrase—strong `transcendental feelings.' For a symbolist-nominalist like Joyce, the problem is less intricate but also less honest, thanks to his Thomist aesthetics: for young Stephen, "the object is *one* integral thing," but it also has a "soul," which "leaps to us from the vestment of its appearance" (*Stephen Hero*, p.213).

75. Originally included in the 1957 edition of *Opus Posthumous* as Stevens' own essay, it is now attributed to the British philosopher H.D. Lewis.

76. This time I am giving this great poem its due consideration and proper reading than was the case in my previous monograph, *Crispin's Voyage*, p. 47.

77. In his essay on John Crowe Ransom (*OP* 259-62), Stevens' description of a poet's relation to ordinary things in life is given with such depth of feeling that his words take on a religious overtone. He starts by describing this relation as "an affair of the whole being" and then continues in this vein: "This is why trivial things often touch us intensely. It is why the sight of an old berry patch, a new growth in the woods in the spring, the particular things on display at a farmer's market, as, for example, the trays of poor apples, the few boxes of black-eyed peas, the bags of dried corn, have an emotional power over us that for a moment is more than we can control" (p.260). Although it is here stated in ostensibly aesthetic terms, nevertheless Stevens' description addresses itself to what Nathan Scott refers to as the modern poet's urge to give to ordinary things their due "ontological weight and depth"; an urge which, as he examines it in greater depth in his essay "Heidegger's Vision of Poetry as Ontology," springs from "a very profound kind of piety," from the modern poet's innermost need "to regard the whole of reality as sacramental" (*Poetics of Belief*, pp.14,167,168). As Stevens himself confesses in one of his letters, "The feeling of piety is very dear to me" (*L* 32), and it is precisely this kind of piety that Scott alludes to.

78. As passionately self-avowed nominalists, Pound and Williams reject Stevens' `serene' as a Symbolist verbal fiction; however, both of them aspire to the selfsame state of mind in their own poetry: Williams in "the music of events, of words, of the speech of the people," eventually elevating such music "into an ordered and utilized whole"; and Pound in exhuming and assimilating "alien and ancient voices, cadences, [and] styles" from a "language museum without walls. . .buried in words." For sources of

citations, see Denis Donoghue, "For a Redeeming Language," in *William Carlos Williams: A Collection of Critical Essays*, ed. J. Hillis Miller (Englewood Cliffs, N.J.: Prentice-Hall, 1966), pp.126,127, and Kazin, *An American Procession*, pp.324,326,329.

79. *Wallace Stevens: A Poet's Growth* (Baton Rouge: Louisiana State University Press, 1986), p.64.

80. This points to the crucial and essential difference in the poetics of Stevens and Williams: one discovering the `serene' in the amplification of poetic consciousness through the aesthetic contemplation of objects (Stevens), and the other through his obsessive urge to poetically locate and sanctify their immanental primacy. It is ironic that Williams often states his `objectivist' aesthetic in terms that apply directly to Stevens, as when he says that for him the aim of poetry is "To refine, to clarify, to intensify that eternal moment in which we alone live." Quoted in *Williams: A Collection of Critical Essays*, ed. Miller, p.16.

81. "Absence in Reality: A Study in the Epistemology of the Blue Guitar," *The Kenyon Review* 21 (1959): 554.

82. *Wallace Stevens: Words Chosen Out of Desire* (Knoxville: The University or Tennessee Press, 1984). p.6.

83. See George Bornstein, *Transformations of Romanticism in Yeats, Eliot, and Stevens* (Chicago: University of Chicago Press, 1976), *passim*.

84. Milton J. Bates, *Wallace Stevens: A Mythology of Self* (Berkeley: University of California Press, 1985), p.110.

85. *From Baudelaire to Surrealism*, pp.112,114. Terms such as `transcendence' or `transcendental longing,' when applied to modern poetry become highly relative. For example, Williams' passionate celebration of ordinary and sometimes outright trivial things, could be described as a form of transcendence directed downwards; so that what Nathan Scott says about Stevens as a poet, could apply equally well to Williams: "Stevens is a profoundly religious poet, but he exemplifies a kind of sensibility

for which the direction, as it were, of transcendence is not upward but downward" (*Poetics of Belief*, p.144).

86. *Portable Emerson*, p.7.

87. The words are Carlyle's quoted in Harold Bloom, *Agon: Towards a Theory of Revisionism* (New York: Oxford University Press, 1983), p.149.

88. *Portable Emerson*, p.28.

89. Frank Kermode, "Dwelling Poetically in Connecticut," in *A Celebration*, ed. Doggett and Buttel, p.273. Walt Whitman, grudgingly acknowledged as the father of all modernists, describes this affirmative inner `leap' as "the luminousness of real vision [which] it alone takes possession, takes value. . .expands over the whole earth, and spreads to the roof of heaven." But Henry Miller, like a true epigone, does even better than the old bard: "I knew then, in the space of a few moments, that something was happening to me which apparently did not happen to everyone. It had come without warning, for no apparent reason that I could possibly think of. . .I recall vividly how the exterior world brightened suddenly. . .that Broadway which I hated so, especially from the elevated line. . .this Broadway had suddenly undergone a metamorphosis. . .it became terribly real, terribly vivid. It had acquired a new orientation; it was situated in the heart of the world, and this world which I now seemed able to take in with one grasp had meaning." For sources of citations see *Leaves of Grass and Selected Prose*, ed. Scully Bradley (New York: Holt, Rinehart and Winston, 1966), p.516; and *Sexus* (New York: Grove Press, 1965), p.308.

90. Miller, *Poets of Reality*, p.223.

91. Seduced by its lush, Matissian sensuousness, a great number of Stevens' commentators tend to look at the poem as celebrating a pagan vision of life, overlooking the fact that such a vision is ultimately subverted by the poem's inherent *lacrymae rerum* gloom and dark pessimism, derived from the irrefutable facticity of

human mortality and the death of a great religious metaphysic. Walter Pater provides us with the most insightful description of the spiritual grief lying at the heart of all paganism: "[The] pagan sentiment measures the sadness with which the human mind is filled, whenever its thoughts wander far from what is here and now. . .making the earth golden and the grapes fiery for him. He makes gods in his own image, gods smilling and flowered-crowned . . .He would remain at home for ever on the earth if he could. As it loses its colour and the senses fail, he clings ever closer to it; but since the mouldering of bones and flesh must go on to the end, he is careful for charms and talismans, which may chance to have some friendly power in them, when the inevitable shipwreck comes." See *The Renaissance: Studies in Art and Poetry*, with an Introduction and Notes by Kenneth Clark (London: Collins, 1964), p.196.

92. *Wallace Stevens*, p.85. Bloom also refers to the poem as being "immensely moving" and "my personal favorite in *Harmonium* (p.57).

93. Ibid., p.63. Bloom looks upon Hoon as Whitman's epigone through and through ("a composite of Stevens and Whitman"), whereas I do so only with reference to his poetic regalia and stance as suggested at the beginning of section 25 in *Song of Myself*:

> *We also ascend dazzling and tremendous as the sun,*
>
> *We found our own O my soul in the calm and cool of*
> *[the daybreak.*
>
> *My voice goes after what my eyes cannot reach,*
>
> *With the twirl of my tongue I encompass worlds and*
> *[volumes of worlds.*

94. This, of course, constitutes Wordsworth's central theme in "The Prelude," which Abrams sums up for us eloquently in *Natural Supernaturalism*, p.27: "We need only to unite our minds to the outer universe in a holy marriage, a passionate love-match, and

paradise is ours." Then he proceeds to cite the following quatrain from the poem in support of his valuation:

> For the discerning mind of Man,
>
> When wedded to this goodly universe
>
> In love and holy passion, shall find these
>
> A simple produce of the common day.

95. Stevens expresses his views concerning man's poetic faculty in his quasi-philosophical but nontheoretical essay "Imagination as Value" (*NA* 133-56). He elevates the poetic imagination to a kind of metaphysic, saying that it is our "only clue to reality" and that its value lies in its "unanalysable intuitions" and power to perceive "the opposite of chaos in chaos" (pp.137,149,153).

96. In identifying himself with the poetic figure in "Tea at the Palaz of Hoon," Stevens made the following remark to Norman Holmes Pearson: "You are right in saying that Hoon is Hoon although it could be that he is the son of old man Hoon. He sounds like a Dutchman" (*L* 871).

97. *Poetry and Pragmatism* (Cambridge: Harvard University Press, 1992), p.22. Poirier also cites William James' own definition of a pragmatist as someone who "turns his back resolutely and once for all upon a lot of inveterate habits dear to professional philosophers. He turns away from abstraction and insuffeciency, from verbal solutions, from bad *a priori* reasons, from fixed principles, closed systems, and pretended absolutes and origins" (p.65).

98. LaGuardia, *Advance on Chaos*, pp.38,39. LaGuardia is only partially correct when he asserts that the poems in *Harmonium* "bear(s) witness to the positive side of commitment to a fluid world," but absolutely right when he says that "Emerson's American scholar permeates these early poems" (pp.38,41). An otherwise excellent study of Emerson's and James' influence on Stevens, nevertheless, in choosing to emphasize the creative

energy and multiplicity of the empiricists' universe and thus understating its chaotic randomness, disorder, and flux, LaGuardia often gives a lop-sided and therefore inaccurate view of Stevens' thought and poetry.

99.   Poirier, *Poetry and Pragmatism*, pp.13,18,25.

100. See note 17 above.

101. As a text, "Circles" also attests, beyond any doubt, to Emerson's predominantly perspectivist-modernist mind and apocalyptic thought as highlighted by the following passages cited from the essay in *Portable Emerson*: "Our life is an apprenticeship to the truth that around every circle another can be drawn; that there is no end in nature, but every end is a beginning; that there is always another dawn risen on mid-noon, and under every deep a lower deep opens (p.228); "New arts destroy the old. . .and that which builds is better than that which is built" (p.229); "All that we reckoned settled shakes and rattles; and literatures, cities, climates, religions, leave their foundations and dance before our eyes" (p.234); "The highest of divine moments [is] that they. . . confer a sort of omnipresence and omnipotence which asks nothing of duration" (pp.237-38); "I unsettle all things. No facts are to me sacred; none are profane; I simply experiment, an endless seeker with no Past at my back" (p.238); "In nature every moment is new; the past is always swallowed and forgotten; the coming only is sacred. Nothing is secure but life, the energizing spirit" (p.239); "The one thing which we seek with insatiable desire is to forget ourselves, to be surprised out of our propriety, to lose our sempiternal memory and to do something without knowing how or why; in short to draw a new circle" (p.240).

102. Poirier, *Poetry and Pragmatism*, p.12. The words are John Dewey's quoted by the author.

103. Newcomb, *Literary Canons*, p.64.

104. Poirier, *Poetry and Pragmatism*, pp.19, 25.

105. Ibid., p.28.

106.   *Literary Canons*, pp.48-80.

107.   The poems in *Harmonium* most baffling to critics, both on account of their titles and content, are "The Emperor of Ice-Cream," "Bantams in Pine-Woods," "Frogs Eat Butterflies. Snakes eat Frogs. Hogs Eat Snakes. Men Eat Hogs," and "The Bird with the Coppery, Keen Claws."

108.   Newcomb, *Literary Canons*, pp.53,63. There was, however, one critic, John Gould Fletcher, who made the following prophetic judgement about Stevens's future standing as a poet (*Freeman*, 19 December 1923): "Any reader who will take the trouble to compare `Le Monocle de Mon Oncle' or `Sunday Morning' with Mr. T.S. Eliot's `Waste Land,' or the best work of the Sitwells, or even M. Paul Valéry's `Jeune Parque,' will realize that Mr. Stevens need fear no comparisons with these internationally famous writers. He is head and shoulders above them all. It is true that he, like these others, is an obscure writer. But his obscurity comes from a wealth of meaning and allusion which are unavoidable; and his intention, when we finally do fathom it, it is far clearer and more earnestly pursued than theirs." Quoted in Doyle, *The Critical Heritage*, pp.46-47.

109.   Newcomb, *Literary Canons*, p.63.

110.   Even as late as 1975 Hugh Kenner, an established literary scholar and critic of major modernists (Eliot, Pound, Lewis, Beckett), finds that the best way of dealing with the challenging complexities of *Harmonium* is outright rejection. See "Williams and Stevens," *A Homemade World*, pp.50-90.

111.   Stevens' question and answer read as follows: "What is the poet's subject? It is his sense of the world" (*NA* 121). What *is*, of course, Stevens' `sense of the world' constitutes for me the one major challenge posed by Stevens the poet, in that *his* sense of the world, unlike that of his compeers (Williams, Eliot, Pound, Frost, Hemingway, Faulkner), is impossible to begin to fathom. And it is exactly this difficulty that defines his poetic perspectivism for me.

112. *Literary Canons*, p.78. Newcomb alludes to one of Stevens' favorite precepts in "Adagia" (*OP* 171): "Poetry must resist the intelligence almost successfully."

113. This valuation belongs to Edmund Wilson, quoted in Newcomb, *Literary Canons*, p.79.

114. Ibid., pp.78-79.

115. "Strange Relation: Stevens' Nonsense," in *A Celebration*, ed. Doggett and Buttel, p.228.

116. My allusion here is to T.S. Eliot's famous statement that "there is a logic of the imagination as well as a logic of concepts." See *Anabasis: A Poem by St.-John Perse* (New York: Harcourt Brace, 1949), p.10.

117. Newcomb, *Literary Canons*, p.74.

118. According to Stevens, "The poem is obviously not about ice-cream, but about being as distinguished from seeming to be" (*L* 341). In his reading of the poem, Richard Ellmann takes its title to mean "the force of being, understood as including life, death, and the imagination"; however, throughout his essay, he makes no reference to the poem's philosophical premise ("Let be be the finale of seem") or attempt to discuss its meaning. Unlikely as it may seem, we do find a gloss for the poem's essential premise in the thoughts of one of Saul Bellow's characters: "There could be no doubt that these billboards, streets, trucks, houses, ugly and blind, were related to interior life. . .There were human lives organized around these ways and houses, and that they, the houses, say, were the analogue, that what men created they also were. . .[that] the people who lived here were actually a reflection of the things they lived among." For sources of citations, see "Wallace Stevens' Ice-Cream," in *Aspects of American Poetry*, ed. Richard M. Ludwig (Ohio State University Press, 1962), p.210, and *Dangling Man* (New York: Signet Books, 1965), p.17.

119. Newcomb, *Literary Canons*, p.66.

120. "Stevens' Nonsense," pp.230, 232-33.

121. Scott, *Poetics of Belief*, p.69.

122. Leggett, *Wallace Stevens and Poetic Theory*, p.123.

123. "Poetry is a cure of the mind" (*OP* 176).

124. George Stone Sausay, *The Penguin Dictionary of Curious and Interesting Words* (Harmondsworth, Middlesex: Penguin, 1986), p.143: *logodaedaly*: "literally, word-skill; it can also refer to the ability to coin new words. *Adj.*: logodaedalian."

125. Leggett, *Wallace Stevens and Poetic Theory*, p.125.

126. Bloom, *Wallace Stevens*, p.405.

127. Stevens himself alludes to his innately solipsistic mind when he refers to "Reality as a thing seen by the mind" (*CP* 468), or observes that "The mind of the poet describes itself as constantly in his poems as the mind of the sculptor describes itself in his forms" (*NA* 46). Also Roy Harvey Pearce, in discussing Stevens' poetic sensibility, has this to say: "At the end, or almost at the end, as we have seen, the mind's sole creation was the mind, the revelation that its sole creation was itself." See "Wallace Stevens: The Last Lesson of the Master," in *The Act of the Mind*, ed. Pearce and Miller, p.141.

CHAPTER II

Poetry as Cure

> You are the music / While the music lasts.
>
> T.S. Eliot, "Dry Salvages"

1

The few poems that Stevens wrote between the publication of *Harmonium* and his next major collection *Ideas of Order* (1935) reflect an intense inner crisis and unabated pessimism; and although it was a crisis that eventually was to give to his later poetry its dominant tone and one of its central themes, most of his commentators have persistently avoided coming to critical terms with it.[1] Eventually, it is Stevens himself who, in employing the word `mind' as a synecdochic trope to describe its metaphysical, psychological, and aesthetic ramifications, helps us, to some extent, understand the nature of his inner disunity. Thus, he tropes his conflict variously as "a war between the mind/And sky. . .that never ends" (*CP* 407), a war that constantly echoes the mind's "terrible incantations of defeat" (*CP* 356), a mind which "exists aware of division" and whose "cry" is as piercing as the sound of a "clarion" (*CP* 377). Moreover, it is a mind which, in its endless search for a `cure', discovers that "It can never be satisfied, the mind, never" (*CP* 247).

In canto vi of "Extracts from Addresses to the Academy of Fine Ideas," a typical long poem of Stevens' middle period (1940), we are given an intimate glimpse, almost confessional in tone, concerning the nature and depth of his unresolved disunity:

61

A Cure of the Mind

Of systematic thinking. . .Ercole,
O, skin and spine and hair of you, Ercole,
Of what do you lie thinking in your cavern?
To think it is to think the way to death . . .

What other one wanted to think his way to life,
Sure that the ultimate poem was the mind,
Or of the mind, or of the mind in these
Elysia, these days, half earth, half mind;

He, that one, wanted to think his way to life,
To be happy because people were thinking to be.
They had to think it to be. He wanted that,
To face the weather and be unable to tell
How much of it was light and how much thought,
In these Elysia, these origins,
This single place in which we think the way,
And, being unhappy, talk of happiness
And, talking of happiness, know what it means
That the mind is the end and must be satisfied.

It cannot be half earth, half mind; half sun,
Half thinking; until the mind has been satisfied,
Until, for him, his mind is satisfied.
Time troubles to produce the redeeming thought.
Sometimes at sleepy mid-days it succeeds,
Too vaguely that it be written in character.
                    (CP 256-57)

The three interrelated themes touching upon the life of the mind, voiced in an almost confessional tone in this canto, constitute Stevens' most crucial and far-reaching poetic subjects:

A Cure of the Mind

(a) the ceaseless opposition between sentience and percipience, or sensuousness and mental cognition ('half earth, half mind;/Half sun, half thinking of the sun; half sky'); (b) the rejection of `systematic thinking' or logical thought as dentrimental to intuitive perception and poetic creation; and (c) Stevens' significant precept, strongly empasized in the canto, that the ultimate aim of poetry is inner unity ('the mind is the end and must be satisfied'). With reference to these three themes, and my own reading of the canto, there are two salient points which I wish to stress in particular, since I consider them to be vitally relevant to my central thesis: firstly, the minimal role Stevens assigns to logical thinking in poetry and the creative process; and secondly, if `the mind is the end and must be satisfied,'[2] then it follows that the satisfaction of such a profound urge can only find its fulfillment outside the realm of sensuous or aesthetic experience—a question broached in "Poems of Our Climate," one of Stevens' "most powerful and moving lyrics":[3]

I

Clear water in a brilliant bowl,
Pink and white carnations. The light
In the room more like a snowy air,
Reflecting snow. A newly-fallen snow
At the end of winter when afternoons return.
Pink and white carnations— one desires
So much more than that. The day itself
Is simplified: a bowl of white,
Cold, a cold porcelain, low and round,
With nothing more than the carnations there.

II

Say even that this complete simplicity
Stripped one of all one's torments, concealed
The evilly compounded, vital I

A Cure of the Mind

And made it fresh in a world of white;
A world of clear water, brilliant-edged,
Still one would want more, one would need more,
More than a world of white and snowy scents.
  III
There would still remain the never-resting mind,
So that one would want to escape, come back
To what had been so long composed.
The imperfect is our paradise.
Note that, in this bitterness, delight,
Since the imperfect is so hot in us,
Lies in flawed words and stubborn sounds.
                    (CP 193-94)

The meaning of the poem is quite clear: however effective our aesthetic efforts may be in our trying to convert the surrounding reality into a world of pure beauty—'pink carnations' in `clear water, brilliant-edged'—eventually all such efforts prove to be incapable of helping us to `strip' our `evilly compounded I' of its `torments'; so that in the end all our poetic creations, regardless of how pristine and mind-healing they may happen to be, only make for an `imperfect paradise' that is destined to subsist on `flawed words and stubborn sounds'. On the other hand, the word `torments'—the key trope in the poem—unquestionably reveals the presence of a strong trans- cendental urge for some kind of inner coherence, unity of being, or belief that would lift `the never-resting mind' out of its deep spiritual morass.[4] As Stevens openly confesses in "Extracts from Addresses," the true end of such an urge is:

  To have satisfied the mind and turn to see,
  ....
  And turn to look and say there is no more
  Than this, in this alone I may believe,

A Cure of the Mind

Whatever it may be; then one's belief
Resists each past apocalypse. (CP 257)

What Stevens is hinting at here is what Yeats calls "the land of heart's desire,"[5] which is the self's longing to recapture its lost unity of being,

to feel again
The reconciliation, the rapture of a time,
Without imagination, without past
And without future, a present time. (OP 38)

In Stevens' own words—strikingly similar to those of Yeats'—this attainment of inner unity is for him "a land beyond the mind" (CP 252), a "final order" (OP 101) wherein the mind, now fully reintegrated, exists in:

An expanse and the abstraction of an expanse,
A zone of time without the ticking of clocks,
A color that move[s] *us with forgetfulness.* (CP 494)

In the end, this urge for inner tranquility, the reconciliation of all contraries as the ultimate `cure' for the mind, takes on a religious overtone that verges on the mystical:[6]

He wanted his heart to stop beating and his mind
                    [to rest
In a permanent realization, without any wild ducks
Or mountains that were not mountains, just to
                    [know

   how it would be,
Just to know how it would feel, released from
                    [destruction,
To be a bronze man breathing under archaic lapis,

Without the oscillation of planetary pass-pass,

A Cure of the Mind

Breathing his bronzen breath at the azury centre
[of time.   (CP 425)

For Stevens, it is these fleeting, quasi-religious experiences of a
fully integrated and spiritually heightened self that can truly
tranquilize his `torments of confusion' and provide a healing
cure for `the never-resting mind':

> *moments of awakening,*
> *Extreme, fortuitous, personal, in which*
> *We more than awaken, sit on the edge of sleep,*
> *As on an elevation, and behold*
> *The academies like structures in a mist.* (CP 386)

It is almost impossible for us to say with any certainty what is
the ultimate cause underlying Stevens' `never-resting mind' or
"restlessness of soul";[7] that is, his endless bouts of grief with self
and world that persist throughout his poetry and constitute one
of its major themes. Be that as it may, the fact remains that it is
in such moments of intense `awakening,' or deeply felt psychic
integration—"the ultimate poem [is] the mind" (CP 256)—that
Stevens finds a `cure' for his inner disunity as well as a new and
revitalizing aesthetic for the poems he was to write after
Harmonium. Beyond any doubt, the primary concern of this
radically new verse is to banish deep and unresolved inner
conflicts, particularly his persistent awareness of flux and
fragmentation—a theme that had sustained *Harmonium*
magnificently, but whose "sublimation" could not possibly
"permit of a sequel."[8] But what is even more significant about
Stevens' later verse is that it brings to light his strong desire for a
creative regeneration of his old, defunct poetic self; a desire,
however, that could only be achieved by a relentless and
systematic intensification of new areas of thought and feeling, as
well as by a radical new approach to subject-matter and use of

language; in fact, to such an extreme degree that one has the distinct impression that the sole aim of Stevens' later poetry is to create a new immanence for his old self.[9] In summing up my argument, I wish to stress that Stevens' verse, after *Harmonium*, more intricately perspectivist and obscure than ever, is motivated by a single, driving urge: the need to create and sustain, by the healing power of words, a unified self; in his own words, "*A nature that is created by what it it says*" (*CP* 490; emphasis mine). These words indicate, beyond any doubt, the momentous end that he wanted his poetry to serve after *Harmonium*.[10]

2

As propounded in his later poetry, Stevens' ontologically reintegrated self is predicated on the following four assumptions: (a) conceived as a purely poetic construct, it projects a radically interiorized consciousness devoid of all recognizable human content or meaning; (b) the poetic imagination, or human faculty traditionally involved in creating autonomous aesthetic artifacts (poems) as extensions of human experience, is now turned into an agency that is used solely for nurturing and insulating the self's interiority; (c) likewise, poetic language becomes a vehicle for the sole purpose of augmenting the self's interiorization, turning all extrinsic experiences into poetic tropes or nonhuman figurations; and (d) at its highest moments of poetic apperception or meditative uplift, the mind experiences its ontological rebirth, so that interiority is converted from a purely mental or aesthetic construct to a self-transcendent experience, whereby the mind may be said to have attained a state of secular beatitude. These premises, postulating Stevens' conception of a reborn self as being essentially an act of the imagination, constitute what I consider to be the true matrix of

Stevens' poetics after *Harmonium*; therefore, as such, they require further elucidation, each according to its centrality and weight.

To begin with, it is important to have a description of the kind of interiority or consciousness the perspectivist mind aspires to as a strong buttress against flux and fragmentation:

> *I should readily consider that the most important form of subjectivity is not that of the mind overwhelmed, filled, and so to speak stuffed with its objects, but that there is another* [kind of consciousness] *which sometimes reveals itself on the side of, at a distance from, and protected from, any object,* a subjectivity which exists in itself, withdrawn from any power which might determine it from the outside, and possessing itself by a direct intuition (emphasis mine).

Moreover, the self that emerges from such interiority is totally transcendentalized:

> *For this self, at best or at worst.* there [is] in the final analysis no time, no history, no living-in-the-world, except in imaginative acts *which, when carried all the way, first transform(ed) and then annul(led) time, history, and the world. The mind, the self, however, could maintain to the end its power of postulation* (emphasis mine).[12]

And finally, the voice that is born in and speaks out of such dizzying depths of interiority, becomes:

> . . .*a pure, ideal Voice, capable of communicating without weakness, without apparent effort, without offense to the ear, and without breaking the ephemeral sphere of the poetic universe,* an idea of some self miraculously superior to Myself (emphasis mine).[13]

The mind that nurtures and inhabits such a preciously guarded interior life, manifests a tightly sealed, solitary, and introverted self, totally disengaged from all common human pursuits and larger historical realities that determine public life.[14] As for the practical aspect of this passionately cultivated interiority, it is twofold: in the first place, it shields the self from outer chaos, in Eliot's famous pronouncement, "the immense panorama of futility and anarchy which is contemporary history";[15] and secondly, it provides all the modern "theologians of the poetic imagination"—Malarmé, Pound, Eliot, Rilke, and Stevens—with the one condition indispensable to their common ideal: the passionate and unsullied pursuit of a private "*religio poetae*."[16]

Like Eliot's, Stevens' mind too feeds itself on a wasteland vision of modern life as a "panorama of despair," a "mangled, smutted semi-world hacked/Out of dirt," filled with "a slime of men in crowds" (*CP* 118,119,135); and it is precisely this horror of the modern urban landscape as a Dantesque hell that impels Stevens to find a `cure of the mind' in the consolations of a private `*religio poetae*,' whose ultimate end should hopefully be the attainment of a higher, integrated consciousness or self. However, despite its intense, quasi-religious modalities, Stevens' envisioning of such a higher self, as projected in his later poetry, amounts to nothing more than "an internal mirage created by the words themselves";[17] that is to say, a pure poetic abstraction rather than a palpably integrated living self who, having found the true "perquisites of sanctity" (*CP* 474), manages to cure `the never-resting mind' of its `torments of confusion.'[18]

In cantos i-ii of "Asides on the Oboe," under the rubric "man without external reference" (*CP* 251), Stevens gives us his version of an idealized, reborn self in a series of highly elusive but closely affined poetic figurations:

I

The impossible possible philosophers' man,
The man who has had the time to think enough,
The central man, the human globe, *responsive*
As a mirror with a voice, the man of glass,

A Cure of the Mind

Who in a million diamonds sums us up.
  II
He is the transparence *of the place in which*
He is and in his poems we find peace.
He sets this peddler's pie and cries in summer,
The glass man, *cold and numbered, dewily cries,*
"Thou are not August unless I make thee so."
Clandestine steps upon imagined stairs
Climb through the night, because his cuckoos call.
          (CP 250; emphasis mine)

And in a similar figuration connoting a higher self, that of the transcendentalized "solitary hero" in canto xii of "Examination of the Hero in a Time of War," Stevens strongly underscores its pure ideality:

It is not an image. It is a feeling.
There is no image of the hero.
There is a feeling as definition.
How could there be an image, an outline,
A design, a marble soiled by pigeons?
The hero is a feeling, *a man seen*
As if the eye was an emotion,
As if in seeing we saw our feeling
In the object seen and saved that mystic
Against the sight, the penetrating,
Pure eye. (CP 278-79; emphasis mine)

And finally, in his last poetic figure of this kind, that of "major man" in canto ix of "Notes toward a Supreme Fiction," Stevens tells us that:

          He comes,
Compact in invincible foil, from reason,
Lighted at midnight by the studious eye,

A Cure of the Mind

Swaddled in revery, the object of
The hum of thoughts evaded in the mind.

....

Give him
No names. Dismiss him from your images,
The lot of him is purest in the heart. (CP 387-88)

Such earlier abstract figurations of the human self can never be more than what they actually are: not flesh-and-blood poetic creations depicting an authentically reborn self, but mere mental constructs specifically created in order to express a state of interiority reduced to a pure or ineffable essence beyond human reach.[19] However, at a more practical level, these abstruse verbal fictions may be looked upon as Stevens' five-finger exercises in Symbolist poetics, which he first took up in "The Man with the Blue Guitar" (1937) and finally gave up following his consummate performance in "An Ordinary Evening in New Haven" (1949). At the heart of this Symbolist poetics is the classic technique of aesthetic inversion: the process of transmuting by `the alchemy of the word' external fact into interior essence; in other words, the momentous imaginative enterprise of converting "the exterior of human existence" into "an inward dimension."[20] Moreover, it is Stevens' belief that one of poetry's main challenges lies in "the transposition of an objective reality into a subjective reality" (*OP* 217) because, according to him, "The world without us would be desolate except for the world within us" (*NA* 169). And he states his case by staying close to official Symbolist doctrine:

> *The material world, for all the assurances of the eye, has become immaterial. It has become an image in the mind. The solid earth disappears and the whole atmosphere is subtilized. . .What we see is not an external world but an image of it and hence an internal world* (*OP* 191).

71

A Cure of the Mind

Eventually, a good deal of this type of Symbolist theorizing finds its way, as subject-matter, in many of Stevens' late poems; for example, all thirty-one cantos of his grand opus, the monumental "An Ordinary Evening in Hew Haven," are a set of variations on a single theme: "the poet's search" for "the philosopher's exterior made/Interior," which he undertakes in order to verify the fact that "Reality is a thing seen by the mind" and therefore, as an artist, his sole concern should "never [be] the thing but the version of the thing:/The fragrance of the woman not her self" (*CP* 481,468,332). However, the deeper reason for the Symbolists' and Stevens' own obsessive quest for the `fragrance' of things, rather than their intrinsic quiddity or value, is "the savagery" of their "plainness," the distressing fact that phenomenal reality is made of "Dark things without a double" and that the mind, lost in "a world of objects" devoid of essence, must find refuge in the "transparent dwellings of the self" (*CP* 467,491,466). In the end, this need to give essence to reality ensnares the mind in a spiral of endless cogitations, which results from its drive to establish the exact point where real and unreal, external and internal, the noumenal and the phenomenal, the self and world meet, and thereof find the ground of true being. In the end, totally lost in the intricate maze of its involuted perceptions, Professor Eucalyptus' mind finally comes to the point where it no longer knows—and this is what makes "An Ordinary Evening in New Haven" the dark comedy of epistemological manners that it is—"what is real and what is not" (*CP* 472). As a result, in order to find an exit out of its inner impasse, the mind accepts the sad but incontrovertible fact that the only reality there is is that "composed of the sun": a fact amply verified by our tragic willingness to keep "coming back and coming back/To the real" as our only redemption (*CP* 465,471).

A Cure of the Mind

Still, the true significance of Stevens' `transparent dwellings of the self', as amplified by the rubrics `major' and `central man', is that they provide us with an ultimate, though somewhat diaphanous, portrait of Stevens' later poetic self. `Major man,'[21] an updated version of Hoon, is imaged as "the philosopher's man" "swaddled in revery"; a ponderously fuller poetic being who, no longer seduced by `the comforts of the sun', has now given himself the momentous task of finding the true `perquisites of sanctity'. In his other guise as a transparent central self, `major man' poses as "an abundant/Poet," a "mirror with a voice" who, "Compelled by an innate music" and "deepened speech," "sums us up in a million diamonds." (*CP* 277,387,250). It is this conception of a radically new, `central' poetic self, projected here as a `philosopher's man' intent on attaining some kind of secular holiness, that accounts to a large extent both for the content and distinctive quality of Stevens' later poetry.

Stevens' conception of the poetic self as "central mind"[22] (*CP* 298) constitutes the most important and far-reaching shift of his sensibility after *Harmonium*. It is a shift that is effected by "a marriage of the self with the source of its being,"[23] which means that the center of poetic perception is now moved from external reality to the mind itself, what Stevens calls "the organic centre of responses" (*CP* 279). Stevens enunciates quite clearly this crucial shift in his poetic thinking in "Chocorua to Its Neighbors":

> *My solitaria*
> *Are the meditations of a central mind,*
> *I hear the motions of the spirit and the sound*
> *Of what is secret becomes, for me, a voice*
> *That is my own voice speaking in my ear.* (CP 298)

As inferred from this revealing verse, this shift is pivotal in shaping Stevens' new poetic idiom because it eventually brings about a radical change in the perceptual commitments of the self; which is to say, henceforth the mind will undertake to carry out *only such poetic acts as reflect on it and thus sustain it.* And what is even more crucial, in effectuating this radical shift in the self's perceptual patterns, is that the mind will now proceed to appropriate or employ its poetic perceptions not "as an act of intelligence"—as was the case with the poems in *Harmonium*—but "as an act of grace" (*OP* 39). And taking our cue from this far-reaching redefinition of the poetic act, we can safely say that it makes for the kind of verse that finally *allows Stevens' mind to find its true cure and sought-for secular sanctity.*

3

What accounts for Stevens' radical shift to a totally new mode of poetic perceptibility is his now impelling concern with what he envisions to be the vital `center' of things: an obsessive urge to try and locate the primal origins of self and world;[24] what he calls "the muddy centre before we breathed" which, according to him, constitutes our "immaculate beginning" and therefore the true "centre of our lives" (*CP* 383,382,198). Since I have already discussed in my commentery on "Landscape with a Boat" Stevens' cognitive effort to arrive at the penetralium of reality, I must now consider at some length the aesthetic aspect of his epistemological speculations as they relate to his new poetic mode.

To begin with, in "Effects of Analogy" Stevens defines for us his conception of `central poetry,'[25] stressing in particular its essential difference from Symbolist verse:

The poet is constantly concerned with two theories. One relates to the imagination as a power within him not so much to destroy reality *at will as to put it to his own uses.* He comes to feel that his imagination is not wholly his own *but that it may be part of a much larger, much more potent imagination, which is his affair to try to get at. For this reason,* he pushes on and lives, *or tries to live, as Paul Valery did,* on the verge of consciousness. *This often results* in poetry that is marginal, subliminal. . .*The second theory relates to the imagination* as a power within him *to have such insights into reality as will make it possible for him* to be sufficient as a poet in the very center of consciousness (emphasis mine). (*NA* 115)

In amplifying upon his definition of central poetry, Stevens points out that "The adherents of the central are mystics to begin with," and therefore the composition of such verse entails "an incalculable difficulty." The difficulty Stevens alludes to here is his momentous centralist postulation that "the structure of poetry and the structure of reality are one," an assumption which is founded, according to him, on "a transaction between reality and the sensibility of the poet" (*NA* 115,116,81, *OP* 217).

Taking into account Stevens' definition of central poetry, as well as all the verses cited hitherto relevant to it, we can summarize the essential characteristics of his new centralist poetic as follows: firstly, it prescribes a truly revolutionary and far-reaching function for the imagination, in that it seeks to turn the poetic act from a purely aesthetic process to a tool of epistemological speculation; it achieves this by forcing the mind to view all reality in primal terms as an inaccessible "hermitage at the centre," and to look upon human consciousness as a "mind of minds" or "self of selves" (*CP* 505,254,297). Secondly,

Stevens' centralist mode proceeds to look upon the physical universe as "A new text of the world"—as "A text of intelligent men/At the centre of the unintelligible" whose "meanings" are solely "our own"; which is a stupendously radical refocusing of poetic vision that supposedly allows the poet to place "himself at the centre of reality," where "everything [is] bulging and blazing and big in itself" (*CP* 494,495,205). And lastly, on account of its relentless quest for the primal source of things, the mind itself eventually becomes deeply involved in a rigorous and unsparing process of aesthetic purgation, what Stevens calls *decreation*, and which, as such, constitutes the cutting edge of his centralist poetic.[26]

And yet, however pervasive these characteristics are of Stevens' work as a whole, in the end they tell us very little about his new centralist mode; and this is because they fail to make us understand the true meaning of his assumption that the structure of poetry and reality are one, or to elucidate in what way his newly patented verse goes beyond the `marginal' and `subliminal' Symbolist aesthetic. However, in order to answer these two crucial questions, we must first establish what is the informing poetic impulse behind Stevens' conception of central poetry, and in this respect Stephen Spender provides a most enlightening and valid explanation:

> *In a world of fragmentated values the imagination cannot illustrate accepted doctrines,* cannot refer to symbolic meanings already recognized by the reader, *symbols of the faith he believes in, and imbibed with his education.* Everything has to be reinvented, as it were, from the beginning, and anew in each work (emphasis mine).[27]

The meaning of Spender's observation is quite clear: a truly modern poem, indeed every single poetic act, constitutes a new `immaculate beginning' in poetic creation since, in discarding all past conceptualizations of self and world, the modern poet embarks on a radical `reinvention' of reality through his daring and fecund experimentation with new theme and metaphor. Similarly, like the good and resourceful perspectivist that he is, Stevens undertakes to `reinvent' the world, this time by conceiving it to be `a text at the centre of the unintelligible'—a formidable view of reality which allows him to drastically expand the scope of his perceptions and thereby renew his depleted creative powers. He stresses this last point in amplifying upon the idea of decreation borrowed from Simone Weil:[28]

> *She says that decreation is making pass from the created to the uncreated, but that destruction is making pass from the created to nothingness. Modern reality is a reality of decreation, in which* our revelations are not the revelations of belief, but the precious portents of our own powers (emphasis mine). (*NA* 174-75)

In other words, in opting to now look at reality in purely centralist terms—as an inaccessible `hermitage at the centre' that involves the mind in an endless epistemological quest for the `ding an sich'—Stevens turns the poetic process into a fertile imaginative territory which he ceaselessly explores in poem after poem; and in so doing, he augments the perceptual power, range, and depth of his centralist poetic mode:[29]

> *One poem proves another and the whole,*
> *For the clairvoyant men* that need no proof:
> *The lover, the believer and the poet.*
> *Their words are chosen out of their desire,*
> The joy of language, when it is themselves.
> *With these* they celebrate the central poem,
> The fulfillment of fulfillments, *in opulent,*
> *Last terms, the largest. . .*
> (*CP* 441; emphasis mine)

However, decreation is a dual destructive/creative process for the centralist poetic mind since, in seeking to reach the vital penetralium of things, it must first deterge itself of all its accumulated or defunct poetic images of self and world:[30]

> *Postpone the anatomy of summer, as*
> *The physical pine, the metaphysical pine.*
> *Let's see the very thing and nothing else.*
> *Let's see it with the hottest fire of sight.*
> *Burn everything not part of it to ash.*
> *Trace the gold sun about the whitened sky*
> *Without evasion by a single metaphor.*
> *Look at it in its essential barrenness*
> *And say this, this is the centre that I seek.*
>
> (CP 373)

And the sun, Stevens' supreme poetic symbol for the primal origin of things, is here called upon to purge and thus help the central mind regain its prelapsarian mental purity:

> *Shine alone, shine nakedly, shine like bronze,*
> *that reflects neither my face nor any inner part*
> *of my being, shine like fire, that mirrors nothing.*
>
> (CP 18)

And this invocation is made in order to remind us that:

> *To-morrow when the sun,*
> *For all your images,*
> *Comes up as the sun, bull fire,*
> *Your images will have left*
> *No shadows of themselves.* (CP 198)

Thus, this pre-Adamic purity that seeks to reduce the mind to an aesthetic *tabula rasa*, becomes for Stevens the one absolute prerequisite for the conceiving and writing of central poetry:

A Cure of the Mind

Throw away the lights, the definitions,
And say of what you see in the dark
That it is this or that it is that,
But do not use the rotted names.

....

Throw the lights away. Nothing must stand
Between you and the shapes you take.[31]
(CP 183)

In "The Auroras of Autumn," one of his most complex and inaccessible poems, Stevens uses the lights of the aurora borealis not only to describe the stark meaninglessness of a world divested of all human myth and anthropomorphic projection, but also to express the unsparing reductiveness and purging aftereffect of decreation:[32]

It leaps through us, through all our heavens leaps,
Extinguishing our planets, one by one,
Leaving, of where we were and looked, of where

We knew each other and of each other thought,
A shivering residue, chilled and foregone . . .
(CP 417)

Stevens' centralist-decreative mode finally evolves to what he calls a poetry of `pure reality', a kind of verse that exemplifies, and to some extent validates, his initial assertion that poetry and reality partake of a common structure. We must, therefore, find out on what grounds Stevens makes this momentous assumption, but in order to do so we have first to understand what he means by `pure reality', and the key to such an understanding is found in canto ix of "An Ordinary Evening in New Haven":

A Cure of the Mind

The poem of pure reality, untouched
By trope or deviation, straight to the word,
Straight to the transfixing object, to the object

At the exactest point at which it is itself,
Transfixing by being purely what it is
....
                              with the sight
Of simple seeing, without reflection. We seek
Nothing beyond reality. Within it,

Everything, the spirit's alchemicana
Included, *the spirit that goes roundabout*
And through included, not merely the visible,

The solid, but the movable, the moment,
The coming on of feasts and the habits of saints,
The pattern of the heavens and high, night air.
                    (*CP* 471-72;emphasis mine)

As made evident by what Stevens propounds in these lines, `pure reality' accrues from the imaginative need to see the `real' in double focus; that is, not only as "The eye's plain version" (*CP* 465), but also as something conceived or imaged in the mind; so that eventually, through their ceaseless interface, these two modes of per- ception—the actual and the ideal, the immanent and the transcendent, brute fact and pure essence—become one, validating Stevens' initial premise that the poetic and the real share a common structure.[33] This validation stems from Stevens' deep belief that by conjoining the phenomenal and the noumenal or real and unreal, the poetic imagination achieves one of its highest goals: it converts what was before a "Dark thing(s) without a double," into what has now "Become(s) amassed in a total double-thing" (*CP* 465,472).

And yet, Stevens' premise undergirding his conception of `pure reality' falls—at least in the eyes and ears of the unwary reader—into self-contradiction; in other words, how is it ever possible to get `to the object at the exact point at which it is itself' if we are to include, in what is supposed to be our pure and unmediated perception of it, `the spirit's alchemicana'—that is to say, the imagination's inexhaustible poetic options? It is obvious, then, that what Stevens means by `pure reality' does not refer to a clear and direct perceptual envisioning of what he calls `the solid', but to the poetic fusion of the phenomenal and the noumenal, thing and idea, fact and essence, as connoted by the rubric `the spirit's alchemicana'. Consequently, Stevens' true intent in conceiving a poetry of pure reality is not really to try and arrive at the point at which `the object is itself'—the old epistemological argument—but instead *to use such a conception as a matrix for augmenting the growth of new and powerful poetic tropes.* Seen in this light, then, it becomes quite evident that, in devising his new verse of pure reality, Stevens' aim is to try and find the noumenal in the phenomenal, that is, discover "God in the object" (*CP* 475); and this proves to be an ingenious epistemological ploy, in that it allows his mind to see reality in a double focus, thus permitting his imagination to expand its perceptual range. In other words, by being able to shift his perceptual focus at will, Stevens turns the act of perception into a "creative activity."[34]

As adumbrated in a number of poems, particularly in "Metaphors of a Magnifico" (*CP* 19), "So-And-So Reclining on Her Couch" (*CP* 295), and a few relevant aphorisms in the "Adagia,"[35] Stevens' view of reality is threefold: (a) as the Kantian `thing-in-itself', opaquely impenetrable and therefore alien to the human intelligence;[36] (b) as natural phenomena and material objects empirically apprehended; and (c) "Reality as a thing seen by the mind" (*CP* 468), by which he means the essence of things as discovered in the act of poetic transformation. And he comfirms this trinitarian conception of reality by vividly dramatizing—in almost overtly sexual metaphors—his obsessive epistemological desire to capture the `real':

> *Three times the concentred self takes hold, three times*
> *The thrice concentred self, having possessed*
> *The object, grips it in savage scrutiny,*
> *Once to make captive, once to subjugate*
> *Or yield to subjugation, once to proclaim*
> *The meaning of the capture, the hard prize,*
>   *Fully made, fully apparent, fully found.*[37]   (*CP* 376)

In the end, by employing his triple vision of things as a poetic ploy whereby he allows himself the necessary latitude for shifting or qualifying his meanings at will, Stevens makes all our perceptual determinants of a solidly structured reality totally fluid, so that eventually the epistemological boundaries of what is `real' and `unreal'—at least in the reader's mind—become indistinguishable. As Stevens himself puts it:

> . . .*there is a reality of or within or beneath the surface of*
> *reality. There are many such realities through which poets*
> *constantly pass to and fro, without noticing the imaginary*
> *lines that divide one from the other* (*OP* 213).

One can persuasively argue that Stevens' habit of constantly playing off one mode of reality against another is poetically valid, in that it broadens the scope of his perceptions by augmenting new and powerful tropes; however, by the same token, one can argue back by pointing out that such an intricately balletic way of perceiving reality often degenerates into the kind of gratuitous epistemological ambiguousness which at times vitiates Stevens' poetry by obfusca- ting it beyond repair.[38]

However, in opting to ground his poetry of pure reality in an aesthetic which seeks to conflate our perceptions of what is `real' and `unreal' to such a degree as to annul all sense of a viable reality, Stevens allows his verse to enter a new and far more complex phase of ongoing poetic perspectivism.[39] In other words, in doing away with our traditional or binary method of apprehending and accommodating reality by two distinctively different and well-defined modes of perception, Stevens brings into his poetry a radical new element of obscurity, what a contemporary critic might refer to as *undecidability*, a term specially coined to account for the absence of thematic coherence or continuity in modern poetry:

> *The symbolic evocations generated by words on the page*
> *are no longer grounded in a coherent discourse, so that it*
> *becomes impossible to decide which of these associations are*
> *relevant and which are not. This is the `undecidability' of*
> *the text I spoke of earlier.* [40]

The question of Stevens' poetic indeterminancy—in itself one of the dominant themes among his critics—is touched upon on many occasions, in varying degrees of explicitness or subtle nuance, in his poetry. For example, in "Angel Surrounded by Paysans," where he poses as our `necessary angel' who makes us `see the earth again', Stevens hastens to remind us of the unreal corporeality of his persona and the intricately elusive and indeterminate nature of his poetic art:

> *Yet I am the necessary angel of earth,*
> *Since, in my sight, you see the earth again,*
> *Cleared of its stiff and stubborn, man-locked set,*
> *And, in my hearing, you hear its tragic drone*
> *Rise liquidly in liquid lingerings,*

A Cure of the Mind

Like watery words awash; like meanings said

By repetitions of half-meanings. Am I not
Myself, only half of a figure of a sort,
A figure half seen, or seen for a moment, a man
Of the mind, an apparition apparelled in
Apparels of such lightest look that a turn
Of my shoulder and quickly, too quickly, I am gone?
                                   (CP 496-97)

Finally, Stevens clarifies for us, in poetic terms, his indeterminancy by posing this memorable question at the end of "Montrachet-le-Jardin," concerning the wayward and fugitive ways of his poetic mind:

And yet what good were yesterday's devotions?
I affirm and then at midnight the great cat
Leaps quickly from the fireside and is gone.   (CP 264)

However, taken at its theoretical face-value, Stevens' `undecidability' cannot be said to be the end result of an impersonal and consciously implemented aesthetic, as is in general the case with modernist poetics. Instead it is safer to say that Stevens' poetic indeterminancies have their root in the very structure and temperament of his poetic mind, and specifically in his epistemological obsessions, anxieties, and endless efforts to find what he believes to be the true nature and center of things. In other words, Stevens' undecidability must be looked upon as the salient characteristic of a congenitally perspectivist and involuted mind—as I have so far argued in this essay—and not as constituting a distinct, formulated aesthetic that may be said to account for Stevens' poetic obscurities in general.

Considered in this light, then, we can say that Stevens' own brand of poetic undecidability is best exemplified in what was to be his last major persona: that of a `necessary' angel-poet entrusted with the momentous task of revealing to us the true meaning of `earth', thus helping us recapture our lost spiritual connection with it.[41] However, what needs to be pointed out is that despite his semi-divine guise, Stevens' angel-poet must be seen for what he really is: as only another version of Stevens' ideal concept of the poetic self; as a replica of the `central poet' or `man of transparence' who, `swaddled in revery', `sums us up in a million diamonds'. But what looms clear behind Stevens' new angelic guise is Ludwig Richter, the old `connoisseur of chaos' and master perspectivist, whose mind, always "Too conscious of too many things at once," still continues to be baffled by the intractable "intricacies of appearence" and "complexities of the world" (CP 271,447).

What finally impels an archperspectivist like Richter, at this late stage in life, to join the angelic orders is the knowledge that as an angel-poet of pure reality he can acquire the kind of interiority or amplitude of being that would enable him to combat and expel from consciousness the complexities of self and world that continue to prey on his mind. And the aesthetic that he chooses to devise in order to acquire such an interiority involves what he calls "the reality/Of the other eye"; that is to say, a poetic transformation of external phenomena whereby "The real [is] made more acute by an unreal" and the mind attains "The infinite of the actual perceived" (CP 448,451).[42] But the crucial upshot of Stevens' new angelic vision of things, fuelled as it is by his secret monist longings, is that it allows him to enter:

> . . .*a world that shrinks to an immediate whole,*
> *That we do not need to understand, complete*
> *Without secret arrangements of it in the mind. (CP 341)*

However what is even more important to a self-avowed connoisseur of chaos like Richter, who knows only too well that this "world/Is more difficult to find than the way beyond," is the fact that this new angelically envisaged earth created by the imagination—what he calls, "a calm world,/In which there is no other meaning" (*CP* 446,455)—is attuned to his deepest urges, in that it resolves all dualities by bringing into a final, consummate union mind and reality.

And yet, it seems that the angelic graces do not transplant themselves that well into actual life. Outwardly a stay-at-home burgherly "Ariel" who lives "a quiet normal life" and is "glad he ha[s] written his poems," in reality his angel-poet's inner and outer life is a shambles (*CP* 523,532). At heart "a man/Of the mind" totally immersed in the life of it, and as a result alienated both from himself and the world at large, his days are filled with a "sadness without cause," a fact that makes him constantly ask himself whether he has "lived a skeleton's life,/As a disbeliever in reality" (*CP* 497,502, *PM* 396). And so the self-image that the angel-poet finally creates for himself in order to give a true picture of his inner life, is that of

> . . .*a man in black space* [who]
> *Sits in nothing that we know,*
> *Brooding sounds of river noises;* (*CP* 444)

and thus the only solace that he finds in his angelic solitude is

> *its parade*
> *Of motions in the mind and the heart,*
> ....
> *the imagination's hymns*
> [Wherein he] *sees its images, its motions*
> *And multitude of motions.* (*CP* 439)

And so, like a true perspectivist or `disbeliever in reality', the angel-poet is destined to remain to the end of his grief-filled days a "fictive man"; and as such, his sole cure will be to continue strumming on his `blue guitar' "divinations of angelic thought"—or, what he chooses to call at other times, his "repetitions of half-meanings" uttered in "watery words" (*CP* 335,503,497).

In concluding this part of my essay, I wish to stress that, however significant or poetically viable the ongoing proliferation and constant shifting of Stevens' highly abstract and elusive personas may be, they eventually tell us very little about the true source of his indeterminate meanings and undecidability in general. Therefore, in an effort to locate this source, we must look elsewhere; namely, in Stevens' own radical way of bringing about the disappearence of the privileged human subject that had dominated, until this century, poetic discourse in Western literature.

4

It was Gustave Flaubert who, like a true protomodernist, first conceived the idea of writing a book in purely aesthetic terms, that is, as an act totally devoid of human content or meaning:

> *What seems to me truly worth doing, what I would really like to do, is to write a book about nothing, a book without external props, which could sustain itself by the intrinsic strength of its style. . .a book which would have almost no subject, or at least one in which the subject would be almost invisible, if such a thing was possible* (translation mine).[43]

Partially applied in his own *Bouvard et Pécuchet*,[44] Flaubert's radical notion of writing a book about `nothing' was eventually taken up by literary purists, avant-guard experimentalists, and linguistic innovators who, intent on bringing about `the revolution of the word', made it into one of the major modernist prose genres.[45] However, the point that needs to be stressed concerning Flaubert's ambitious venture is his overtly anti-humanist stance in rejecting the idea of a distinctly human subject in such a literary work, which to him would have been the intrusion of the human condition into pure art. Needless to say, the formulation of his outré project has had a crucial and lasting effect on the large majority of twentieth-century modernist writers: firstly, it helped them eliminate from their work the use of traditional subject-matter; and secondly to radically redefine the nature and function of aesthetic perception in both prose and poetry.[46]

The result of a long historical process, the disappearence of what had always been the major human themes in Western art, particularly in literature, had proceeded in two main stages. Stage one marked the Romantics' break with the humanist tradition, who had sought to alleviate their acute religious crisis by attaching transcendental meanings to physical things and natural phenomena. Georg Simmel sums up this Romantic process very cogently:

> *Even the lowest, intrinsically ugly phenomenon appears in a context of colours and forms, of feelings and expe- riences that bestow upon it a fascinating significance. We only need to involve ourselves deeply and lovingly enough in the most indifferent phenomenon—that in isolation is banal or repulsive—in order to be able to conceive of it too as a ray or symbol of the ultimate unity of all things, from which beauty and meaning flow and for which every philosophy, religion and moment of our most heightened emotional experience seeks out symbols. If we pursue this possibility of aesthetic preoccupation to its conclusion, we find that there no longer exists any distinction between the amount of beauty in things. Our world view becomes that of aesthetic pantheism. Every point conceals the possibility of being released into absolute aesthetic significance. To the*

> *adequately trained eye, the total* beauty, *the* total
> *meaning of the world as a whole radiates from every single*
> *point.*[47]

Stage two sets in as soon as Romanticism begins to lose its urge
to spiritualize things—it tended to look at a "blade of grass" as if
it "breath[ed] a cryptic message"[48]—and gradually gives its place
to Realism as the new dominant art movement. But the realist
writers too brought with them their own aesthetic shibboleths
and obsessions: first, their lumpen vision of life and manic fetish
with materiality; and second, their stylistic assumptions and
militant views concerning the social ends of art in general. In the
end, as a result of their compulsive need to cram their novels
and plays with endless catalogues and inventories of things in
describing the material interiors and exteriors of a new and
rapidly urban milieu, they began to compromise the autonomy
of art and thus diminish its power for self-renewal through free
and creative experimentation. It is only natural that the initial
and unanimous reaction of the early modernists against the
excesses of realism would be to "deliver art from the dead weight
of the object"[49] and have it "replaced by abstraction and
artifice."[50] However, as a result of their own fetishistic
preoccupation with in-depth perception, collagist constructions,
and perspectival distortions of visual reality, what the modernist
artists, as a whole, eventually succeeded in doing was to turn the
Romantics' transcendentalized object into an "anti-object"; which
is to say, they now appropriated and used physical objects for
purely artistic purposes, and, in so doing, inevitably reduced
them to mere "texture" or pure form.[51]

    With regard to early modernist verse, the aftereffects of
`the revolution of the word' were equally levelling and far-
reaching. According to Valery, his idea of `pure poetry' could be
best materialized by turning all verse into "a system of relations
unconnected to the practical order" of ordinary life, thereby

reducing each individual poem into an autonomous aesthetic microcosm in which "*the play of figures contained the reality of the subject*" (emphasis mine).[52] Also, Pound's own need to radically do away "with the binary opposition between verse and prose"—which he used as an organizing principle in his own *Cantos*—eventually made for a poetic that tended, by its own aesthetic logic, to reduce all cultural history and personal biography to a bewildering collagist jumble of "*objects trouvés* that relate only equivocally to the discource in which they are embedded."[53] In practical poetics, this means that "the image of man," as projected in early modernist verse, had been reduced to "a complex of [aesthetic] forces,"[54] and the poet's own speech to "a pure nameless voice breathing [its words] into the air"; that is to say, a voice which, having "learned to extricate itself from the surrounding man,"[55] was now able to keep "the reader at arm's length and. . .not allow itself to be human."[56] In sum, as Donald Davie points out, the tendency of modernist verse since the time of Rimbaud has been to make both the syntax and subject-matter of poetry appeal "to nothing but itself, to nothing outside the world of the poem."[57]

But the main reason for the final break of modernist verse with traditional poetry was its self-reflexivity; and, predictably enough, it was Rimbaud who, as the true pathfinder of the modernist poetic interior, first made his follow poets aware of this new aspect of the modern mind, by declaring that "It is wrong to say *I think*. One ought to say *I am being thought*."[58] It was left, however, for Valery to systematize the implications of Rimbaud's cogito and eventually formulate them into a self-sealed aesthetic in which the poetic act is asked to sustain itself by its own interior processes. Stephen Spender elucidates upon this very point with the added insight of the creative artist:

> *The mode of perceiving itself becomes an object of perception, and is included as part of the thing perceived.*

> [Modern artists] *do not just analyse the structure of objects, they also impose on the object the simplifying, abstracting, yet multifold way of seeing things which is their own.*[59]

Ultimately, what Valery aspires to achieve by pure poetry is total artistic self-sufficiency, in fact not unlike the kind that Flaubert had hoped to attain by writing a book about `nothing'. According to Valery, the ideal `pure' poem should be a consciously constructed verbal artifact of such refined perfection that it could, conceivably, perpetuate itself by feeding on its own aesthetic autonomy. As he puts it:

> *The* [pure] *poem. . .does not die for having lived: it is expressly designed to be born again from its ashes and to become endlessly what it has just been. Poetry can be recognized by this property, that* it tends to get itself reproduced in its own form (emphasis mine).[60]

However, in addition to its pervasive introvertedness, there is an equally strong perspectivist dimension in Valery's poetic theory,[61] hinted at by Spender's remark about the modern artist's `multifold way of seeing things'—an observation whose implications are clarified for us by Valery himself:

> *Poetry's special aim and own true sphere is the expression of what cannot be expressed in the finite functions of words. The proper object of poetry is* what has no single name, what in itself provokes and demands more than one expression. That which, for the expression of its unity, arouses a plurality of expressions (emphasis mine).[62]

Taking into consideration Valery's central role in the transition from late symbolism to early modernism, his recognition of perspectivism as one of the dominant elements of modern verse is of great significance, in particular his insight as to the way the modernist mind works; according to him, a mind

A Cure of the Mind

. . .in which the transmutation of thoughts into each other appeared more important than any thought, in which the play of [poetic] *figures contained the reality of the subject.*[63]

Looking back now at the masterworks of the modernist poetic canon from Rimbaud to John Ashbery, it becomes quite obvious that the common aim of their creators was to heal their shattering experience of the modern world through the invention of a radical poetic idiom; or according to two contemporary scholars of literary modernism, by turning their inner personal crisis into a passionate preocupation with artistic experiment.[64] Thus, given their obsession with theory and compulsion to privatize their meanings, we can say that the one poetic subject all modernist poets were attuned to were "the figurations of [their own] mind"[65] and nothing more; and the reason for this was because, for most of them, that was the only place which could provide "an inaccessible [and] ideal boundary [for] the poet's desires, efforts, and powers."[66]

Stevens' conception of poetry as a cure for the mind's disjunctions must be considered within the framework of such developments as outlined above; more specifically, it must be assessed within the context of his own persistent efforts, following the publication of *Harmonium*, to find the true subject of his poetry in the very `figurations' and `play' of his own mind as suggested by Valery.[67] The first step he had to take in achieving his goal was to reject all humanist or anthropomorphic stances associated with traditional verse; that is, to radically disavow "any personal identification with an object. . .as a mirror of humanity"[68]—a rejection he had already voiced in "Nuances of a Theme by Williams" (1918), and which he was to reconfirm in even stronger terms many years later in "Less and Less Human, O Savage Spirit" (1944).[69] It seems, then, that in the twelve-year interim between *Harmonium* and his second collection *Ideas of Order*, Stevens had already begun to evolve a new poetic mode as evidenced by the disorienting disconnectedness and near-solipsistic ruminations of "Like Decorations in a Nigger Cemetery" included in the latter volume.[70] This new mode, which was to become increasingly dominant as time wore on, is based on Stevens' precept, borrowed from Henri Focillon, that "The chief characteristic of the mind is to be constantly describing itself," a process which Stevens applies to poetic creation as well (*NA* 46). Leaving aside the question of false analogy in Stevens' argument, what this belief really amounts to is an attempt to justify, in purely conceptual terms, the actual workings of his own poetic mind and the deeper urges that prompt them. What he is saying in essence is that, for him, his true poetic subject lies in the very process of the poetic act itself; that is, in the actual aesthetic, psychological, and ontological experiences that accrue from the writing of poetry, in total disregard to the historical, social, or common human events that lie outside the thinking, feeling, and creative intensities of the poetic act itself.

Stevens' definitive statement as to where his true poetic subject lies is voiced strongly and unequivocally in the widely quoted and much discussed first half of canto xxii in "The Man with the Blue Guitar":

> *Poetry is the subject of the poem,*
> *From this the poem issues and*
> *To this returns. Between the two,*
> *Between issue and return, there is*
> *An absence in reality,*
> *Things as they are. Or so we say.*   (*CP* 176)

The three closely interrelated propositions which make up the argument of the poem—and whose true meaning continues to elude Stevens' critics to this day[71]—not only help us understand the principle at work in the composition of "The Man with the Blue Guitar" itself,[72] but also provide us with the necessary key in fathoming the nature and use of Stevens' intricate tropes as exemplified in all his longer poems, from "The Comedian with the Letter C" (1922) to "An Ordinary Evening in New Haven" (1950). What the opening couplet of this canto tells us clearly is that a poem's true subject is the poet's impelling urge for poetic expression, and that this urge is inseparable from, or identical with, his actual experience of the poetic process itself:

> *The poem is the cry of its occasion,*
> *Part of the res itself and not about it.*
> *The poet speaks the poem as it is.*   (CP 473)

Thus, according to Stevens, the poem as an aesthetic artifact and the poet's experience in creating it—poem as both objective fact and subjective experience—eventually become indistinguishable.[73] This interpretation is fully borne out by his own paraphrase of the first proposition that `poetry is the subject of the poem':

> *Poetry is the spirit, as the poem is the body. Crudely*
> *stated, poetry is the imagination. But here poetry is used*
> *as the poetic, without the slightest pejorative innuendo. I*
> *have in mind pure poetry. The purpose of writing poetry is*
> *to attain pure poetry* (L 363-64).

As Stevens points out, `poetry' here refers to the imagination in general, but more specifically to the actual poetic process or imaginative activity ('spirit') that creates the actual poem, and which process, according to him, constitutes the poem' true `subject' as distinguished from its purported or formal subject, what he calls the `body' of the poem. And for Stevens, it is out of this interactiveness of the poetic process, the journey `between issue and return', that a poem is born and enables us to transcend our human nausea with `things as they are'; and if, somehow, the solace that comes with the joy of poetic creation is suspended, then we find ourselves, once again, thrown back into `a world without imagination,' which is Crispin's own spiritual plight.[74]

But to say that a poem's subject and the poetic act that materializes it constitute an aesthetic continuum, the idea that "Poetry and materia poetica are interchangeable terms" (*OP* 159), not only does injustice to Stevens' complex mind but also forgoes the true meaning of his paraphrase; and the key word here that can help us unravel that meaning is `spirit'. As applied to Stevens' poetry and thought, the word derives its special significance from what he calls `the spirit's alchemicana' (which I have already discussed in connection with Stevens' conception of central poetry), and as such it addresses itself to Valery's principle of pure poetry, which is the unlimited and gratuitous "play of the mind and sensibility over a topic."[75] In other words, Stevens' involuted phrase refers to the propensity of his mind to constantly engage itself in the creation of poetic figurations or tropes as a means of providing a poem with what he considers to be its true subject; in fact to such an extreme degree that eventually "the mind's processes become the poet's patterns";[76] which is to say, at one point the subjects of his poems and the act of troping them become indistinguishably one.

What needs to be stressed at this point, by way of elucidating further upon the full implications of the proposition `poetry is the subject of the poem', is that Stevens' identification of poetic subject with troping goes beyond what one might call the calculating strategies of a predetermined or applied aesthetic. In reading Stevens' later poetry, one has the distinct feeling that each individual poem is "created in an act of consciousness, not reality";[77] in other words, his poems give the impression of having been written in order to fill an ontological void, which Stevens reexperiences as `an absence of reality' as soon as he ceases to write verse. We must, then, look upon Stevens' uninhibited use of poetic troping or `free play of the mind and sensibility' as a vital imaginative "activity" that helps him "discover(s) another dimension of his being,"[78] and which activity he refers to as `candor'; therefore, according to him, it is only the poem which, fully augmented by radical and powerful troping, "can bring(s) us a power again," that is,

> *the strong exhilaration*
> *Of What we feel from what we think, of thought*
> *Beating in the heart, as if blood newly came,*
> *An elixir, an excitation, a pure power.   (CP 382)*

It is through such intense ontological experiences (or `elixir'), augmented by the mind's exuberantly profuse and richly inventive tropes,[79] that Stevens is able to give a revitalizing glow to his inner self; and the only way for him to do so is by allowing his mind to become engaged in an obsessive epistemological quest to find "the very center of consciousness" (*NA* 115)—which is his endless effort to establish a viable definition for `the poem of pure reality'. Thus, looked at from a strictly ontological angle, it becomes increasingly obvious that Stevens' overreaching tropes (whereby the `mind' extends itself `beyond the range of the mind')[80] become directly instrumental in turning his longer poems into the kind of intense and unfocused self-meditations whose underlying impulse is to augment and sustain a process which Lawrence Lipking refers to as "soul-making."[81] In underscoring the significance of Lipking's observation, we can say that all of Stevens' epistemological searchings, his `visions and revisions' with regard to what is `real' and `unreal', are only an excuse that allow him to work to the outermost limits of its imaginative power; and thus, through the creative joy of his prodigious tropings, help him find his true `perquisites of sanctity'—his one and only cure.

A Cure of the Mind

Looking once again at Stevens' famous tercet (cited earlier on), it is now obvious that the word `occasion' refers not only to the inner urge that impels Stevens to write a new poem, but also to his need to make its subject one with his troping. This interpretation is warranted by the contexualized meaning of the word `cry', which is here used as a synecdoche for the actual experience of poetic troping per se; that is, with "the very process of thinking, feeling, [and] imagining enacted"[82] in the poem, and which process Stevens refers to as `the res itself'; and the Latin word is used here as a synecdote for the whole poem as both subjective experience and objective artifact. At this point it is relevant to mention Stevens' practice of making his aesthetic doctrine part of his subject-matter, as made clear by his assertion that "We do not prove the existence of the poem" (*CP* 440) since, for him, "The poem is the poem, not its paraphrase" (*L* 362) and therefore `the poet speaks the poem as it is'. The point Stevens wishes to stress here is that, by definition, a poem is nonparaphrasable because its meaning is determined by the very troping that enacts that meaning; since, however, in its highest poetic purity troping is an ineffable experience,—"a nonlinguistic phenomenon"[83]—the meaning that it carries in a poem cannot be transcribed in rational terms through conventional language. Thus, if "*the revelation of reality* is inherent in the words"[84] of a poem (*OP* 213) then, however complex or inaccessible that poem's tropes may happen to be, it is their inviolate verbal purity that finally ensures and validates for Stevens their effectiveness as a cure of the mind:

> *The curtains, when pulled, might show another whole,*
> *An azure outre-terre, oranged and rosed,*
> *At the elbow of Copernicus, a sphere,*
> *A universe without life's limp and lack,*
> *Philosopher's end. . .What difference would it*
> *   [make,*

97

A Cure of the Mind

So long as the mind, for once, fulfilled itself?
(OP 91)

5

"Of Modern Poetry," Stevens' poetic manifesto in verse, provides us with the best single text yet for understanding his conception and usage of poetic tropes:

> *The poem of the mind in the act of finding.*
> *What will suffice. It has not always had*
> *To find: the scene was set; it repeated what*
> *Was in the script.*
> *   Then the theatre was changed*
> *To something else. Its past was a souvenir*
> *It has to be living, to learn the speech of the place.*
> *It has to face the men of the time and to meet*
> *The women of the time. It has to think about war*
> *And it has to find what will suffice. It has*
> *To construct a new stage. It has to be on that stage*
> *And, like an insatiable actor, slowly and*
> *With meditation, speak words that in the ear,*
> *In the delicatest ear of the mind, repeat,*
> *Exactly, that which it wants to hear, at the sound*
> *Of which, an invisible audience listens,*
> *Not to the play, but to itself, expressed*
> *In an emotion as of two people, as of two*
> *Emotions becoming one. The actor is*
> *A metaphysician in the dark, twanging*
> *An instrument, twanging a wiry string that gives*
> *Sounds passing through sudden rightnesses,*
> *   [wholly*
> *Containing the mind, below which it cannot*
> *   [descend,*

A Cure of the Mind

Beyond which it has no will to rise.
It must
Be the finding of a satisfaction, and may
Be of a man skating, a woman dancing, a woman
Combing. The poem of the act of the mind.
                    (CP 239-40)

Personified into the dual figure of `actor' and `metaphysician,'
the poem deals with the role of poetry in the modern age,[85] and
in particular with the fate of the modern poet: a man for whom
the past is now a `souvenir' and thus finds himself living in a
world that has the look of a deserted theater. And so, burdened
with his own bleak vision of `things as they are', he consoles
himself by `twanging on a wiry string', at the same time
occupying his mind with the momentous task of trying `to find
what will suffice'. So conceived, the poem's actor-metaphysician
is one of Stevens' minor perspectivists, a poetic persona that
looks backwards to its great prototype, the guitar-playing verbal
wizard in "The Man with the Blue Guitar," and forward to
Ludwig Richter's agonized mind and totally destructured world.

As for the rubric `poem of the mind' and its variant, `act
of the mind,'[86] it is only another name for the poem of pure
reality' and therefore, as a cognate poetic artifact, it addresses
itself to `the spirit's alchemicana'; that is, to that selfsame
creative process whereby Stevens' imagination, by means of the
fullest possible `play' of its intricate tropes, converts the
phenomenal `real' into the numinous `unreal', and by so doing
allows the mind to come by its new `revelations of reality.'
Since, however, we are not given the slightest hint as to what the
`poem of the mind' is really after—what would `suffice' for it, or
what its newly discovered revelations ultimately portend—we
finally come to realize that its undefined quest is only another

patented Stevensian ploy, in that what it really `discovers'[87] are its own tropes:

> But to impose is not
> To discover. To discover an order as of
> A season, to discover summer and know it,
>
> To discover winter and know it well, to find,
> Not to impose, not to have reasoned at all,
> Out of nothing to have come on major weather.

The meaning of these lines from "Notes toward a Supreme Fiction" is quite clear: the `revelations' that the `poem of the mind' eventually discovers are the very tropes and figurations with which it fleshes out itself; because, in actual fact, these tropes—what Stevens refers to here as `major weather'—are born of the poet's radical perceptions which he brings to bear on his fierce desire to rediscover primal `summer' and `winter', as recorded in "Credences of Summer" and "The Snow Man."[88] In short, the revelations that ultimately accrue from the `poem of the mind' are identical with the poet's own primal insights and epiphanies about `summer' and `winter', as engendered in the very process of conceiving and writing his mind poem. At this point, it is appropriate to mention that Stevens himself is quite aware of the fictive or purely verbal nature of a poet's—or his own—'revelations': "Poetry is a revelation in words by means of the words," and therefore "A poet's words are of things that do not exist without the words" (*NA* 32,33).

But what is even more significant is the fact that Stevens' poet-metaphysician, as conceived and projected in "Of Modern Poetry," chooses to compose his mind poem `in the dark';[89] which is to say, all his essential perceptions, tropes, and insights come to him unexpectedly like divinations; that is, as if they were "moments of awakening,/Extreme, fortuitous, personal, in which/We more than awaken" (*CP* 386). What this means is that, for Stevens, our innermost perceptions come into being in a purely discontinuous and random fashion; like intuitive flashes unimpeded by the inner checks of rational thought or the aesthetic exigencies of a larger poetic framework.[90] It is this very irrational, disjunctive fortuitousness, the act of writing `in the dark' whereby we come by our `moments of awakening', that constitutes the essential nucleus of the mind poem as espoused in "Of Modern Poetry." Once again, "Notes toward a Supreme Fiction" provides the appropriate gloss:

> *On the image of what we see, to catch from that*
> *Irrational moment its unreasoning,*
> *As when the sun comes rising, when the sea*
> *Clears deeply, when the moon hangs on the wall*
>
> *Of heaven-haven. These are not things*
>   *[transformed.*
> *Yet we are shaken by them as if they were.*
> *We reason about them with a later reason.*
>   (*CP* 398-99)

These lines tell us how Stevens' mind comes to its `irrational' tropes, as well as offer us an apologia for their poetic use. `Difficultest rigor' refers to the great imaginative effort required by `the spirit's alchemicana', the process by which we convert what we optically see in an object ('sun', `sea', `moon') into an image in the mind; and what we choose to see in that object—as depicted in the image Stevens calls `moment'—is our mystical or `irrational' apprehension of it.[91] As for the word `unreasoning', it is addressed to the radical and disjunctive tropes we need to invent in order to transcribe our irrational experience of the object, and whose own illogicality, allowed either by aesthetic necessity or poetic licence, is at par with the nature of that experience. Finally, we `reason about' our seemingly illogical perceptions and poetic transformations with `a later reason'; that is, by a subsequent act of logical analysis or rational explanation. As for Stevens' apologia concerning the aesthetic justification for such poetic or mystical experiences and the irrational troping they give rise to, the best gloss, once again, is found in the "Notes":

> *They will get it straight one day at the Sorbonne.*
> *We shall return at twilight from the lecture*
> *Pleased that the irrational is rational.*
>
> (*CP* 406)

However, what is of greater relevance concerning Stevens' theory of tropes as set forth in "Of Modern Poetry" is their privileged priority and overpowering presence in his work, which totally subverts the vital role that predetermined subjects once played in the creative process; in fact, to such a high degree, that the question itself as to what may now be said to constitute a legitimate subject for poetry is, to say the least, a matter of pure chance. As Stevens puts it, "the choice of subject-matter is a completely irrational [and] fortuitous thing," that is, something that "poets. . .find on the way." In other words, according to him, ultimately our most precious "acquisitions of poetry" are "*trouvailles*," that is, the things that we come across `in the dark' as we compose our `poem of the mind' (*OP* 220,193,169). It must, however, be pointed out that Stevens' notion or fortuity as a vital element in modern poetry—the idea that a poem may be "organized out of whatever material one can snatch up" (*L* 361)—has its source in Valery; according to whom the subject of a `pure' poem ought to be "completely irregular, inconstant, involuntary, and fragile," that is, something that "we find by accident."[92] Likewise, for Stevens the question of choosing a subject for a poem is a matter of pure chance, something which "depends"—as he characteristically puts it—"on a walk around a lake" (*CP* 386); which is to say, a poem may be triggered off by a totally insignificant event or fleeting visual impression: `a man skating, a woman dancing, a woman combing'.[93]

As expounded in "Of Modern Poetry," Stevens' theory of fortuity is radically subversive. What he tells us in certain terms is that the first thing a modern poet should try to understand and accept, in mastering what is to be a rigorously probing and hard-edged verse, is that, eventually, "one subject is as good as another,"[94] and that, having divined the true essence of that fact, he finally comes to realize that the true meaning of what he chooses to write about resides solely in `the play of his mind and sensibility', which is to say, in the very tropes and figurations he invents in fleshing out his poems. In the end, what such discoveries teach the modern poet is that the creative impulse responsible for his figurations ultimately has its origin not in the aesthetic object under contemplation, but in the inner needs of his own mind.[95] As I have already pointed out in my commentary on "The Poems of Our Climate," no matter how aesthetically appealing or inspiring an object may happen to be for Stevens—in this case, `pink and white carnations' in `clear water'—it finally proves to be incapable of providing a lasting cure for his "torments of confusion" (*CP* 27) or `evilly compounded I'. In other words, whatever it is that ails his `never-resting mind', it is quite obvious that the remedy his inner disarray requires is not to be found in the pristine beauty of pink and white carnations in clear water, or in some self-shattering mystical experience;[96] rather, if such a remedy could be said to exist, it would most likely be found in the mind's ontological renewal, augmented by a ceaseless flow of new and powerful tropes and other feats of metaphorical language.

A Cure of the Mind

This interpretation of "The Poems of Our Climate" is made valid by Stevens' abiding belief that "the mind is the end and must be satisfied" (*CP* 257), a belief that falls into line with his conception of poetry as propounded in "Of Modern Poetry," and is encoded in that cryptic phrase dangling at the end of the poem. The meaning tagged onto this final, encapsulating label-phrase—the `poem of the act of the mind'—is the poem of total, inordinate, and fiercely radical troping that seeks to go `beyond the range of the mind', and whose goal therefore is not the creation of perfect poetic artifacts but the miraculous acquisition of inner integration. And this ardently sought after `unity of being', according to Stevens, can only be attained by those uncompromisingly free, spontaneous, and overreaching cogitations carried out `in the dark'—violent poetic self-acts whose effect on the mind is so overpowering and liberating, that in the end they become what Stevens, quite appropriately, calls `perquisites of sanctity'. The true essence of this telling phrase is that it reveals to us the vital role that radical tropes play in his poetry, as well as the extent to which he depends on them as a source of spiritual sustenance and inner unity. Thus, according to him, "one writes poetry in order to approach the good in what is harmonious and orderly"[97] (*OP* 222); or, as he confesses in what must have been a moment of acute inner need, "one writes poetry in order to find God" (*OP* 220). In the end, the redemptive power of poetic perception becomes for him an ontological matrix by which he conceives and defines the very meaning of his own personal existence: "I have no life except in poetry" (*OP* 175).

Yet even more crucial is Stevens' impassioned dependence on his `moments of awakening' or poetic divinations, what Harold Bloom calls "transcendental bursts of radiance";[98] experiences which have as their common theme the mystical awareness of a higher level of consciousness or self and therefore, on account of their intensity, allow Stevens to momentarily regain his unity of being and thereof reconfirm the healing power of the poetic imagination. Moreover, it is Stevens' belief that this mystical apperception or "establishing of a [higher] self" (*NA* 50) is the result of an "occasional ecstasy of the mind" (*NA* 35), and therefore "no less a degree than the experience of the mystic" (*NA* 50-51). Finally, on account of the inner impact of such ecstatic `moments', we are "born/Again" (*CP* 321) "Without the labor of thought" (*CP* 248) "at the end of distances" (*CP* 527), where the mind, now immersed in a "vivid transparence of peace" (*CP* 321), can.

> *feel again*
> *The reconciliation, the rapture of a time*
> *Without imagination, without past*
> *And without future, a present time. . .*[99]
> (*OP* 72)

In canto i of "Prologues to What Is Possible," Stevens fully amplifies upon this vision of a mystically integrated mind which, having reached what appears to be a state close to beatitude, now rests `in a permanent realization at the azury centre of time':

> *I*
> *There was an ease of mind that was like being alone in*
> * [a boat at sea,*
> *A boat carried forward by waves resembling the bright*
> * [backs of rowers,*
> *Cripping their oars, as if they were erect on the wooden*
> * [handles,*
> *Wet with water and sparkling in the one-ness of their*
> * [motion.*

A Cure of the Mind

The boat was built of stones that had lost their weight
                              [and being no longer heavy
Had left in them only a brilliance, of unaccustomed
                                                    [origin,
So that he that stood up in the boat leaning and looking
                                          [before him
Did not pass like someone voyaging out of and beyond
                                          [the familiar.
He belonged to the far-foreign departure of his vessel
                              [and was part of it,
Part of the speculum of fire on its prow, its symbol,
                              [whatever it was,
Part of the glass-like sides on which it glided over the
                                          [salt-stained water,
As he travelled alone, like a man lured on by a syllable
                              [without any meaining
A syllable of which he felt, with an appointed sureness,
That it contained the meaning into which he wanted
                                          [to enter,
A meaning which, as he entered it, would shatter the
                              [boat and leave the oarsmen quiet
As at a point of central arrival, an instant moment,
                                          [much or little,
Removed from any shore, from any man or woman, and
                                          [needing none.
                    (CP 515-16)

In the final analysis, Stevens' poetic mystifications must be seen
for what they really are: inner projections of a deeply alienated
and transcendentally inclined mind, which craves for "the deeper
harmonies"[100] as "A healing point in the sickness of the mind"
(OP 112). Moreover, these quasi-mystical projections of self and
world have as their source Stevens' lifelong inner conflict: on the

one hand his dark, despairing conviction that "There is no such thing as life" (*CP* 192), and on the other, his obsessive need to always want to transcendentalize life's spiritual poverty into a "Total grandeur of a total edifice" (*CP* 510), so that his spirit may continue to live with `things as they are'. Thus, for Stevens, the only viable way to eradicate this abysmal discrepancy between inner need and outer reality is to adopt a private and ennobling ideal—an act which stems from his deep awareness that "there is nothing outside of the mind to feed on as value," and that therefore "one feeds on one's own desire for order."[101] It may well be that the modern poet's inner search for such `deeper harmonies', and the methods he adopts in reaching them, follows a pattern that is similar to that of the mystic's own quest.[102] The fact remains, however, that the goals of the poet and the mystic point to radically opposite directions: the mystic, when finally confronted with the ineffable, must proceed to jettison his cogito and all the labyrinthine bypaths of human feeling, thought, and language;[103] in other words, he must renounce the very tools the modern poet vitally depends on in the course of his own momentous quest to rediscover and define for us, through the power of poetic speech, our true immanence—an immanence which, according to Williams, lies in our ability to "smell, hear and see afresh with a new language."[104] What is ironic, however, about Williams' view of language as constituting our most authentic way of recovering and celebrating our earth-bound humanity, is that it is superceded by Stevens' far more radical belief, which is the power and ontological efficacy of words—a belief that sets him apart from his poetic peers, including Williams. This belief rests on Stevens' deep conviction that the very meaning of our most profound discoveries of self and world—whether related to our human immanence or our innermost transcendental longings—is ultimately contingent upon, and therefore coterminous with, the words we use to express such `discoveries'. As Stevens himself puts it very clearly: "A poet's words are of things that do not exist without the words" (*NA* 32), a precept that applies equally well to our more mystical `moments' since, according to him, we eventually realize that "words become the words/Of an elevation, an elixir" (*OP* 83).

It is quite obvious, then, that the primary aim of Stevens' poetry is not the recovery and celebration of the vital sources of life, as is decidedly the case with Williams' humanist-oriented poetics; rather, Stevens' own primary objective is the self's ontological renewal or `elevation' as enacted within the creative process itself. This takes us back to Stevens' conception of poetry as an act of the mind—an act which, by fomenting intense poetic mystifications, allows the mind to regain its `deeper harmonies' or inner unity. The reason, then, that Stevens' mind is so partial to strong imaginative tropes, is because they are vitally involved in initiating and augmenting such intense mystifications, and as a result create a higher inner music:

> . . .*a savage and subtle and simple harmony,*
> *A matching and mating of surprised accords,*
> *A responding to a diviner opposite.*
> (*CP* 468)

In other words, it is as if, seduced by the incantatory intensity of its own tropes, Stevens' mind is elevated to a new plane of inner harmony, wherein he finally attains what he calls "catalepsy" (*CP* 397), or his "daily majesty of meditation" (*CP* 518). And this is the state of mind Joseph Riddel alludes to when he says that Stevens' tropes allow him to "possess the world"[105] anew, or Harold Bloom implies when he claims that tropes provide Stevens with "a therapy in which consciousness heals itself by a complex act of invention."[106]

A Cure of the Mind

The great paradox, however, with Stevens' mystical envisionings of self and world is that, as the inner pressure for them increases, so does the violence and complexity of his tropes; as if, by some strange alchemy of mind, Stevens' mystifications draw their power and appeal—to quote Hillis Miller once again—from his `unpredictable, savage, and violent voice'. Be that as it may, the fact remains that Stevens' tropes constitute the most distinctive and authentic element of his poetic sensibility; that is, the true `perquisites' of his `sanctity' which, as the creative agents of his inner music, allow him to have access to `a diviner opposite' and thereof a lasting cure for his `never-resting mind.' And as such, they are the true source of that `unpredictable and savage voice' that Miller is so intent on finding out where it finally `comes from' and how we should listen to it.[107]

NOTES

1.   With reference to the nature and possible source of Stevens' inner crisis, Helen Vendler offers this theory: "Many of Stevens' poems—read from one angle, most of the best poems—spring from catastrophic disappointment, bitter solitude, or personal sadness. It is understandable that Stevens, a man of chilling reticence, should illustrate his suffering in its largest possible terms. That practice does not obscure the nature of the suffering, which concerns the collapse of early hopeful fantasies of love, companionship, success, and self-transformation. As self and beloved alike become, with greater or lesser velocity, the final dwarfs of themselves, and as social awareness diminishes dreams of self-transcendence, the poet sees dream, hope, love, and trust—those activities of the most august imagination—crippled, contradicted, dissolved, called into question, embittered. This history is the history of every intelligent and receptive human

creature, as the illimitable claims on existence made by each one of us are checked, baffled, frustrated, and reproved—whether by our own subsequent perceptions of their impossible grandiocity, or by the accidents of fate and chance, or by our betrayal of others, or by old age and its failures of capacity." See *Part of Nature, Part of Us: Modern American Poets* (Cambridge, Mass.: Harvard University Press, 1981), pp.41-2.

2. Already at 26 Stevens believed the mind to be the sole source of personal fulfillment and inner unity: "We get figures of speech, and impressions, and superb lines, and fantastic music. But it's the mind we want to fill—with Life" (*SP* 167).

3. See also my discussion of this poem in my previous monograph, *Crispin's Voyage*, pp.20-2.

4. For a study of the religious and transcendental strains in Stevens' poetry, see Adelaide Kirby Morris, *Wallace Stevens: Imagination and Faith* (Princeton, N.J.: Princeton University Press, 1974), *passim*.

5. Quoted in Kathryn R. Kremen, *The Imagination of Ressurection: The Poetic Continuity of a Religious Motif in Donne, Blake, and Yeats* (Lewisburg: Bucknell University Press, 1972), p.285.

6. See my previous monograph *Crispin's Voyage*, p.23.

7. Vendler, *Words Chosen Out of Desire*, p.40. For Hillis Miller, Stevens' `restlessness' expresses itself through "self-division, contradiction, and perpetual oscillations of thought" (*Poets of Reality*, p.258), whereas for Bloom it is due to the fact that "the mind never sleeps until death" (*Wallace Stevens*, p.291). It is George Poulet, however, who makes the essential connections concerning Stevens' chronic `restlessness' and grief; according to him, modern man's *tristis casus* is due to the fact that, having lost his "divine immanence," he lives in "an insupportable void" which

he must try to fill by "a perpetual renewing of the heart [and mind]," or some secular "zone of joy and total light." See *Studies in Human Time*, trans. Elliot Coleman (Baltimore: The Johns Hopkins Press, 1956), pp.10,18,29,54. For a quasi-medical view of Stevens' poetic mind as pathologically suspect, see Jascha Kessler, "Wallace Stevens: Entropical Poet," *The Wallace Stevens Journal* 1 (1977):82-86.

8. Fletcher, quoted in Doyle, *The Critical Heritage*, p.47.

9. In the sense that our notion or experience of self is contigent upon consciousness. See *Philosophical Dictionary*, compiled and edited by Walter Berger and Kenneth Baker (Spokane, Wash.: Gonzaga University Press, 1974), p.191.

10. Stevens' conception of poetry as `cure' goes beyond I.A. Richards' theory of synaesthesis or reconcilliation of conflicting impulses. However, inasmuch as Richards' theory may be said to involve the "whole of man" (or artist), whose sole aim is to look "into the heart of things" and so be able "to lift away the burden of existence"—then we can say that synaesthesis does address itself to some important elements in Stevens' poetics of self. See "I.A. Richards: A Poetics of Tension," in William K. Wimsatt and Cleanth Brooks, *Literary Criticism: A Short History* (New York: Knopf, 1957), pp.616-20.

11. Georges Poulet quoted in Lentricchia, *After the New Criticism*, pp.65-6.

12. Pearce, "Last Lesson of the Master," p.138.

13. Paul Valery, "Poetry and Abstract Thought," *The Art of Poetry*, with an Introduction by T.S. Eliot (New York: Vintage Books, 1961), p.81. As part of his critique of phenomenology, Derrida

provides us with the best interpretation yet of the "phenomenological voice" as enunciated here by Valery: "It is not in the sonorous substance or in the physical voice, in the body of speech in the world but in the voice phenomenologically taken, speech in its transcendental flash, in the breath, the intentional animation that transforms the body of the world into flesh, makes of the *Körper a Leib, geistige Leiblichkeit*. The phenomenological voice would be this spiritual flesh that continues to speak and be present to itself—*to hear itself*—in the absence of the world." Quoted in Lentricchia, *After the New Critisism*, pp.72-3. Amplifying further upon Derrida's critique of the `phenomenological voice' as a logocentric fiction, Lentricchia correctly points out, referring to Proust's work as a case in point, that although its `voice' may conceptually be proven a fiction, nevertheless the essence or `truth' of *Remembrance of Things Past*, "considered as the totality of the manifestations of the person" can never be denied (pp.79-80).

14. At 26 Stevens had already considered solitary existence to be the one absolute precondition for the life of the mind and poetic creation: "I long for Solitude, not the solitude of a few rooms, but the solitude of self. I should like to make music of my own, a literature of my own, and I should like to live my own life" (*L* 79-80). It is, however, Mallarmé who provides the classic example of a totally self-sealed mind exclusively devoted to poetic creation: "The life which surged round him at this period is the same that rolls tumultuously through the novels of Zola—the Second Empire, the war, the Commune: at thirty he was fairly well acquainted with Paris, London, and the life of the French provinces: and of all this he retains nothing for his work." See Stéphane Mallarmé, *Poems*, translated by Roger Fry with Commentaries by Charles Mauron (New York: New Directions, 1951), p.16.

15. *Selected Prose*, ed. Frank Kermode (London: Faber and Faber, 1984), p.177. As for Stevens' own view of history as a humanist

myth or value, his rejection is categorical: "the vast mausoleum of human memory is emptier than one had supposed" (*NA* 101). Stevens' rejection of history is in keeping with the anti-historicist stance of Emerson and Ortega y Gasset, two visionary perspectivists who believe that "There is no history" because man, being "the entity that makes itself," constantly "stands in need of a new revelation." See LaGuardia, *Advance on Chaos*, p.37, and Ortega, *History as System and Other Essays* (New York: Norton, 1961), pp.201,223.

16. Michael Hamburger, *The Truth of Poetry: Tensions in Modern Poetry from Baudelaire to the 1960s* (Harmondsworth, Middlesex: Penguin, 1972), p.112. Stevens too looks upon poetry as a kind of "mystical theology" (*NA* 173) and the poet as a "monastic man" (*CP* 382). However, it is Henry James who gives us an inside view of the almost quasi-mystical ecstasy experienced in tending to one's private `religio poetae': "To live in the world of creation—to get into it and stay in it—to frequent and haunt it—to think intensely and fruitfully—to woo combinations and inspirations into being by a depth of continuity of attention and meditation—this is the only thing" (*SCB* 73).

17. Julian Barnes, in a review of Mallarmé's published letters, *New York Review of Books*, 9 November 1989, p.10.

18. It may be that such envisionings of self-regeneration are imaginatively more feasible in fiction, as is the case with Lawrence's parables of self-resurrection. Be that as it may, of all modern poets, Eliot comes closest to a convincing envisioning of a spiritually reborn self in *Four Quartets*.

19. Stevens' idea of the self as pure `transparence' has definitely its origin in Emerson's `transparent eyeball' as a trope for clairvoyant interiority: "Standing on the bare ground—my head bathed by the blithe air and uplifted into infinite space—all mean egotism

vanishes. I become a transparent eyeball; I am nothing; I see all" (*Portable Emerson*, p.11).

20. Maurice Blanchot, *L' Espace littéraire* (Paris: Gallimard, 1955), p.175. As Stevens himself once put it in underlying his Symbolist affinities, "The imagination takes us out of reality into a pure irreality" (*L* 360). It is a poetic creed totally opposed to that of Williams' who fiendishly adheres to the belief that, "No symbolism is acceptable. No symbolism can be permitted to obscure the real purpose, to lift the world of the sense to the level of the imagination and give it new currency." Quoted in Richard Ruland and Malcolm Bradbury, *From Puritanism to Postmodernism: A History of American Literature* (London: Routledge, 1991), p.241. Also, for an account of Williams' outrage and rejection of "Description without Place," one of Stevens' most abstruse, quasi-Symbolist poems, see Alan Filreis, *Wallace Stevens and the Actual World* (Princeton, N.J.: Princeton University Press, 1991), pp.181-83.

21. Bates chooses to read `major' man as Stevens' version of Nietzsche's overman (*Mythology of Self*, pp.234-65). In my estimation, such a view could be taken as pure fabrication or an act of willful misreading—in either case, a valuation contrary to all internal evidence in the canon. As a rule, Stevens' poetic selves are conceived as a "crystal hypothesis" (*CP* 387), interiorized essences beyond all human identity or meaning, a stance that applies in this case as well: "The major men. . .are neither exponents of humanism nor Nietzschean shadows. . .The major men are part of the entourage of that artificial object (poetry)" (*L* 485).

22. In his persistent efforts over the years to have us believe that Stevens' poetic roots go back to Whitman, Emerson, and the English Romantics, Bloom chooses to give to his reading of `central man' an Emersonian twist, thus refusing to relate the term to Stevens' cognate notions of `central mind', `central self',

`central poetry'. However, had he decided to give to his reading of `central man' its proper focus, he would have had to radically revise his theoretical stand. See "The Central Man: Emerson, Whitman, Wallace Stevens," *The Ringers in the Tower: Studies in the Romantic Tradition* (Chicago: University of Chicago Press, 1971), pp.217-33.

23. C.Roland Wagner, "Wallace Stevens: The Concealed Self," *The Wallace Stevens Journal* 12 (1988):98.

24. Stevens' obsession with the primal origin of things, also reflected in his desire in the late 40s to establish in great depth his family tree, is movingly voiced in his poem "The Irish Cliffs of Moher":

> *Who is my father in this world, in this house,*
> *At the spirit's base?*
> *My father's father, his father's father, his—*
> *Shadows like winds*
> *Go back to the parent before thought, before speech,*
> *At the head of the past.*   *(CP 501)*

For further discussion see Bates, *Mythology of Self*, pp.279-92, and Thomas F. Lombardi, "Wallace Stevens and the Haunts of Unimportant Ghosts," *The Wallace Stevens Journal* 7 (1983):46-53.

25. Stevens' major critics—Pearce, Vendler, Riddel, Miller, Bloom—pay scant attention to the poems that have as their theme Stevens' conception of center and centrality, mainly because—one is tempted to suspect—such poems do not happen to fit their set approaches to Stevens' poetry. For a critical discussion of such poems, see Carroll, *A New Romanticism*, pp.199-200, 260-69.

26. For a more detailed discussion of decreation in its aesthetic, cognitive, and epistemological aspects, see my previous monograph *Crispin's Voyage*, pp.13-30.

27. *The Struggle of the Modern* (London: Hamish Hamilton, 1963), p.50.

28. A true godsend for most Stevens scholars, the idea of decreation has been used and abused to critical death, in the same way that Eliot's `objective correlative' was by his own commentators in the 40s and 50s. Stevens employs the term here extemporaneously to describe the process of aesthetic reduction, common to all modern art forms as a necessary precondition for artistic experimentation and creative renewal.

29. In general, Stevens' critics fail to focus on the true relevance of his epistemological speculations for what they really are: a way of augmenting powerful and original poetic tropes. Thus, a literary scholar of Riddel's stature can say unabashedly that "Poetry is an epistemological adventure for Stevens because life is" (*The Clairvoyant Eye*, p.28).

30. As Stevens once remarked to a fellow correspondent about the art of poetry: "The object is of course to purge oneself of anything false" (*L* 636). B.J. Leggett focuses on the true meaning and aesthetic function of decreation when he says that, "What is crucial in Stevens' assumption about the creation of poetry is that it can begin only at the point where the world [is] reduced to zero and [becomes] amenable to the distinct and unique language of the poet" (*Wallace Stevens and Poetic Theory*, p.123).

31. This is how Hillis Miller describes the unsparing single-mindedness with which the decreative poet puts to work his stark, reductionist aesthetic: "He must throw out, for example, what science, mythology, theology, and philosophy tell him about the sun and see the sun as the first man saw it for the first time. . .
To perceive the sun, the poet must forget all about Phoebus and forget the very name of the sun. Nothing must come between him

and the sun when he gives himself to the act of looking at it and seeing it for the first time" (*Poets of Reality*, p.248).

32. As Stevens himself puts it, "These lights symbolize a tragic and desolate background" (*L* 852), and the `background' alluded to here refers both to our demythologized view of the physical universe and the reductive aftereffect of decreation.

33. In "To an Old Philosopher in Rome," Stevens' elegy for George Santayana, the ambient physical reality is seen through this double focus of the immanent and the transcendent, an approach appropriate to the subject of the poem. As Merleau-Ponty points out in commenting on Cezanne's painting: "Essence and existence, imaginary and real, visible and invisible—a painting mixes up all our categories in laying out its oneiric universe of carnal essences, of effective likenesses, of mute meanings." Quoted in Leonard and Wharton, *The Fluent Mundo*, p.12.

34. Margaret Peterson, *Wallace Stevens and the Idealist Tradition* (Ann Arbor. Mich.: UMI Research Press, 1983), p.23.

35. "The real is only the base. But it is the base"; "The ultimate value is reality"; "Realism is a corruption of reality"; "Reality is a vacuum"; "Reality is the motif"; "The full flower of the actual, not the California fruit of the ideal"; "Reality is the spirit's true center"; "There is nothing in the world greater than reality"; "Reality is a cliché from which we escape by metaphor" (*OP* 157-80).

36. In *Critique of Pure Reason*, Kant points out that "As appearances, they [external phenomena] cannot exist in themselves, but only in us. What objects may be in themselves, and apart from all this receptivity of our sensibility, remains completely unknown to us." See Peterson, *Wallace Stevens and the Idealist Tradition*, p.23.

A Cure of the Mind

37. Bloom (*Wallace Stevens*, p.251) believes that these lines describe "the triple process" or "dialectic" of Stevens' poetry; he chooses, however, to interpret this dialectic in terms of his own `anxiety-of-influence' theory.

38. The poems I have in mind in making this valuation are as follows: "Description without Place" (*CP* 339); "This Solitude of Cataracts" (*CP* 424); "Bouquet of Roses in Sunlight" (*CP* 430); "The Bouquet" (*CP* 448); and parts of "An Ordinary Evening in New Haven" (*CP* 465).

39. There is a great deal of paradox and intellectual pathos in Stevens' poetic transformations: inasmuch as he needs to sustain himself by constantly decreating reality by converting the actual `real' into the imaginative `unreal' and vice versa, in the end he finds the inner strain unbearable; and then what he wants is for his "mind to rest/In a permanent realization/. . . at the azury centre of time"; or, as he puts it in another poem, what he craves for is "A gaiety of being" "Without the labor of thought" (*CP* 425, 248).

40. Marjorie Perloff, *The Poetics of Indeterminancy: Rimbaud to Cage* (Princeton, N.J.: Princeton University Press, 1981), p.22.

41. There are strong Rilkean undertones in Stevens' conception of the `necessary angel' as a symbol of pure being and visionary guardian of `earth'. As the German poet said once to his Polish translator: "The angel of the Elegies is that creature. . .who guarantees the recognition of a higher level of reality in the invisible." See *Selected Poetry*, p.317. For a discussion of Rilke's poetic angels, see H.F.Peters, *Rainer Maria Rilke: Masks and the Man* (New York: McGraw-Hill, 1963), pp.120-57.

42. There is also a close parallel between Rilke's process of poetically internalizing all external phenomena, what he calls inwardness (*Innerlichkeit*), and Stevens' constant counterposing of the real

(sense datum) with the unreal (its imaginative simulacrum or essence). For a discussion of Rilke's concept of poetic inwardness, see Eudo C.Macon, *Rilke* (London: Oliver and Boyd. 1963). pp.17-22, 88-91.

43. Letter to Louise Colet, January 16, 1852: "*Ce qui me semble beau, ce que je voudrais faire, c' est un livre sur rien, un livre, sans attache extérieure, qui se tiendrait de lui-même par la force de son style. . .un livre qui n' aurait presque pas de sujet ou moins où le sujet serait presque invisible, si cela se peu.*" See *Correspondance*, II, (Paris: Gallimard, 1980), p.31.

44. "A nameless work" whose aim was to prove "the nothingness of human intelligence" or "l'eternelle misère de tout," Flaubert's last novel was finally foiled by its very subject. According to one of his contemporary critics, the book is "A purely philosophical work. Nothing could be less like a novel." See Maurice Nadeau, *The Greatness of Flaubert*, trans. Barbara Bray (LaSalle, Ill.: Open Court Publishing, 1973), pp.267,275.

45. The most notable contributions to the genre, both on account of their content and `metalanguage', are Paul Valery's *Monsieur Teste*, James Joyce's *Finnegans Way*, Gertrude Stein's *Tender Buttons*, Samuel Beckett's novels, and Raymond Queneau's *Exercises du Style*.

46. In saying this I have in mind Pound's great admiration for Flaubert's prose style, which he used as a model in formulating his own Imagist poetics.

47. Quoted in Frisby, *Fragments of Modernity*, p.57.

48. Friedrich Holderlin and Eduard Mörike, *Selected Poems*, trans. Christopher Middleton (Chicago: The University of Chicago Press, 1972), p.xxxvii.

49. Casimir Malevich quoted in Wylie Sypher, *Rococo to Cubism in Art and Literature* (New York: Vintage Books, 1963), p.312.

50. Robert Smithson quoted in Marjorie Perloff, *The Futurist Moment: Avant-Garde, Avant-Guerre, and the Language of Rupture* (Chicago: The University of Chicago Press, 1986), p.xviii.

51. Sypher, *Rococo to Cubism*, pp.325,322.

52. Valery, *The Art of Poetry*, pp.189,192.

53. Perloff, *The Futurist Moment*, p.192. It is worth mentioning that Rilke also refers to the poems in his *Neue Gedichte* as `thing poetry'; it is therefore necessary that an essential distinction be made at this point. Pound is liable, on account of his rigorously applied Imagist/Objectivist poetic, to reduce all human experience and material objects to mere aesthetic artifacts; Rilke, Williams, and Francis Ponge, on the other hand, engage their full poetic sensibility in recovering and celebrating the nonhuman—or to them inviolate and enduring—immanence of things. In his discussion of Ponge's poetry, Hugo Friedrich makes this distinction quite clear: "The subjects of his free verse poems are called bread, door, shell, pebble, candle, cigarettes. They are captured so factually that one critic (Sartre) has spoken of a `lyrical phenomenology'. The ego that captures them is fictitious, a mere carrier of language. This language, however, is anything but realistic. It does not so much deform things as make them so inert, of impart so strange a vitality to things inert by nature, that a spooky unreality is created. But man is excluded." Quoted in Hamburger, *The Truth of Poetry*, p.32.

54. Sypher, *Rococo to Cubism*, p.322.

55. José Ortega y Gasset, *The Dehumanization of Art and Other Writings on Art and Culture* (Garden City, N.Y.: Anchor Books, 1956), pp.29-30.

56. Hugo Friedrich quoted in Ernst Fischer, *The Necessity of Art: A Marxist Approach* (Harmondsworth, Middlesex: Penguin, 1963), p.70.

57. Quoted in Hamburger, *The Truth of Poetry*, p.25

58. Quoted in Fischer, *The Necessity of Art*, p.91.

59. *The Struggle of the Modern*, pp.132-33.

60. *The Art of Poetry*, p.72.

61. Ultimately, what informs Valery's poetics too is the precept that "The world is a structure of variable relationships and multiple appearances," the fact that with the discovery of every "new perspective" we become more aware that "there is no perspective." And this precept applies equally well to modernist fiction; for example, Gide conceived and wrote his *Les Faux Monnayeurs* on the principle of "continual discontinuity" and "'creative incoherence'," that is, the idea that "'every new chapter should pose a new problem, serve as a new beginning, a new impulse, a plunge ahead'." See Sypher, *Rococo to Cubism*, pp.273,277,307.

62. *The Art of Poetry*, p.177.

63. Ibid., p.192.

64. Ruland and Bradbury, *From Puritanism to Postmodernism*, p.175.

65. Sypher, *Rococo to Cubism*, p.319.

66. Valery, *The Art of Poetry*, p.192.

67. Riddel describes Stevens' own poetic introversion as "an aspect of mind bound by its ambience" (*The Clairvoyant Eye*, p.23), and relates it to Croce's intuition-expression theory.

68. Kenneth Burke, "William Carlos Williams: Two Judgments," in *Williams: A Collection of Critical Essays*, ed. Miller, p.56.

69. See also my discussion of Stevens' rejection of pathetic fallacy in *Crispin's Voyage*, pp.15-17.

70. A poem that has stubbornly resisted meaningful interpretation to this day, Stevens once described it to a fellow correspondent as "litter," that is, a collection of random apercus "written on the way to and from the office" (*L* 272).

71. Although Riddel takes his fellow critics to task for having "regularly confused [these] first three couplets," his own interpretation of them—to the effect "that the act of poetry is a thing in itself"—is equally unconvincing (*The Clairvoyant Eye*, p.144). On the other hand, Bloom admits that the canto is "most problematic" and proceeds to read it in the light of his own set theorizations; he does say, however, that "perspectivism is the mark of nearly all the imagery of [cantos] xxii through xxvii" (*Wallace Stevens*, p.131). As for Vendler, she eschews any meaningful discussion of the canto in her long analysis of "The Man with the Blue Guitar" (*On Extended Wings*, pp.119-43).

72. Vendler's valuation of "Like Decorations in a Nigger Cemetery" could be said to apply to all of Stevens' longer poems: "If this is a poetry of meditation, it does not have the sustained progressive development that we know in other meditative poets; it is rather the staccato meditation of intimation and dismissal, of fits and

starts, revulsions and shrugs, lightenings and sloughs" (*On Extended Wings*, p.71).

73. The greatest single obstacle in the New Critics' approach to Stevens' poetry, and in particular his intricate use of tropes, is their own restrictive view of the ideal poem as a tightly organized, self-sealed verbal construct. As a case in point, see R.P.Blackmur's essay "Examples of Wallace Stevens," in *Wallace Stevens: A Critical Anthology*, ed. Ehrenpreis, pp.59-86.

74. The best gloss for Stevens' dictum "Reality is a vacuum" (*OP* 168) is voiced by Eryximachus in Valery's *Dance and the Soul*: "If our soul purges itself of all falseness. . .of every fraudulent addition to *what is*, our existence is at once endangered by this cold, exact, reasonable, and moderate consideration of human life as it is. . .*to see things as they are*. . .is a poison impossible to combat. The real, in its pure state, stops the heart instantaneously." See *Dialogues*, trans. William McCausland Stewart, with Two Prefaces by Wallace Stevens (London: Routledge and Kegan Paul, 1957), pp.51,52.

75. Vendler, *On Extended Wings*, p.71.

76. Lensing, *A Poet's Growth*, p.109.

77. Helen Regueiro, *The Limits of Imagination: Wordsworth, Yeats and Stevens* (Ithaca: Cornell University Press, 1976), p.186.

78. Riddel, *The Clairvoyant Eye*, p.49.

79. Although Ruland and Bradbury are correct in saying that "The underlying aspiration" in Stevens' work is "epistemological," that is, it reflects "a desire to capture in words, to create with words, not so much the meaning of experience as the act of seeking that meaning," they fail to point out the strong creative urge and joy

that attends such games with poetic meaning. See *From Puritanism to Postmodernism*, p.341.

80. The reference here is to Stevens' extraordinary statement cited in the opening paragraph of Chapter 1. I want to believe that I have managed to locate its true meaning and context in relation to his thought and poetry.

81. *The Life of the Poet: Beginning and Ending Poetic Careers* (Chica- go: Chicago University Press, 1981), p.7.

82. Hamburger, *The Truth of Poetry*, p.27.

83. Leggett, *Wallace Stevens and Poetic Theory*, p.130.

84. For a commentary on the full implications of Stevens' contention, see Appendix for my reading and analysis of "Not Ideas about the Thing but the Thing Itself".

85. According to George Bornstein (*Transformations*, pp.2,4) "Of Modern Poetry" constitutes "a miniature treatise on modern poetics," which "exemplifies its own tenets." However, he makes the totally unfounded claim by saying that it is "a poem of earth" whose "radical humanism" confirms the Romantic origins of Stevens' poetry.

86. These are two of Stevens' patented poetic labels that have generated the most theorizing, critical controversy, and confusion among his commentators, mainly because their true import and relevance to his poetry and thought seems to escape them. Stevens probably had in mind Samuel Alexander's phrase "the act of mind" (*OP* 193).

87. Clauco Cambon correctly describes Stevens' "poetry as a process of dialectical discovery; he does not, however, proceed to say what it is that Stevens' dialectic eventually `discovers'. See *The Inclusive Flame: Studies in Modern American Literature* (Bloomington, Ind.: Indiana University Press, 1965), p.137.

88. As Riddel points out, it may be that behind Stevens' strong urge to rediscover `primal summer' lies the need "to fill the void," or "to establish the discreet primacy of mind over things" (*The Clairvoyant Eye*, p.194). His observation, however, still leaves unanswered the question as to why Stevens has to use such illogical tropes in order to arrive at his discovery.

89. See also canto xxxii in "The Man with the Blue Guitar": "Throw away the lights, the definitions,/And say of what you see in the dark" (*CP* 183).

90. Hillis Miller looks at Stevens' `irrational' tropes in the right context: "If a poem is to be true to life it must be a constant flowing of images which come as they come and are not distorted by the logical mind in its eagerness for order" (*Poets of Reality*, p.261). On the other hand, Denis Donoghue not only rejects Stevens' disorienting tropes but his poetry as a whole, on the ground that it lacks "accredited meanings." See "Stevens' Gibberish," *Reading America: Essays on American Literature* (New York: Knopf, 1987), p.169.

91. With regard to poetry, for Stevens the two words are interchangeable: "Pure poetry is both mystical and irrational" (*OP* 222).

92. *The Art of Poetry*, p.60.

93. Stevens has borrowed these cameos from Charles Mauron: "All his poems [Mallarmé's] have an extremely concrete starting-point: the

furniture of a bedroom, the curtains of a window, a girl diving, a woman combing her hair" (*Mallarmé: Poems*, p.31).

94. Flaubert quoted in *Documents of Modern Literary Realism*, ed. George J. Becker (Princeton, N.J.: Princeton University Press, 1963, p. 93. The full quotation runs as follows: "In literature there are no fine artistic subjects. . .and consequently one subject is as good as another." This is what Stevens wishes to emphasize when he describes a poem variously as a "meteor," "prayer," "café," "pheasant," or "*trouvaille*" (*OP* 158-73).

95. In referring to Stevens' cameos ('a man skating, a woman dancing, a woman/Combing'), and asking the question "What these have to do with acts of mind?" (*Transformations*, p.5), Bornstein gives us to understand that (a) he does not quite know what Stevens means by `acts of mind', and (b) fails to see their close connection with Stevens' views concerning the importance or function of `subjects' in poetry. In short, what he fails to understand is that there are no poetic subjects as such for Stevens, since, anything is capable of triggering off an aesthetic response for him at any given moment. As Frank Lentricchia correctly points out, "For Stevens a scene, an object, is only a starting-point for a voyage into [poetic] abstraction" (*The Gaiety of Language*, p.132).

96. As a true progenitor of twentieth-century literary illuminists, Flaubert was the first to experience profound divinations at the sight of an ordinary object: "Often, catching sight of something or other—a drop of water, a shell, a hair—you stopped and stood quite still, your gaze transfixed, your heart opened." Quoted in Jephcott, *Proust and Rilke*, p.16. Profound as they may be, all such experiences ('illuminations', `visions', and `epiphanies'), as manifested in the work of all the major modernist writers—Joyce, Proust, Woolf, Pound, Eliot, and Stevens—must be accepted for what they really are: the quasi-religious flareups or secret longings of the post-Christian mind in crisis. Walter Pater gives us the true content and spiritual tenor of such visionary experiences:

"Revelation, vision, the discovery of a vision, the seeing of a perfect humanity, in a perfect world—through all his alternations of mind, by some dominant instinct, determined by the original necessities of his own nature and character, he had always set that above the *having*, or even the *doing*, of anything. For such vision, if received with due attitude on his part was, in reality, the *being* something, and as such was surely a pleasant offering or sacrifice to whatever gods there might be, observant of him" (*Marius the Epicurean*, p.378).

97. In a letter to Alfred A. Knopf (May 25, 1954), Stevens had requested that his forthcoming collected poems be entitled *The Whole of Harmonium*. This request was eventually turned down by Knopf (*L* 834).

98. *Ruin the Sacred Truths: Poetry and Belief from the Bible to the Present* (Cambridge, Mass.: Harvard University Press, 1989), p.200.

99. Stevens' lines echo Eliot's own in "Burnt Norton," *Four Quartets* (London: Faber and Faber, 1970), p.13:
    Time present and time past
    Are both perhaps present in time future,
    And time future contained in time past.
    If all time is eternally present. . .

100. George Santayana, *Interpretations of Poetry and Religion* (New York: Harper Torchbooks, 1957), p.6.

101. Eugene Paul Nassar, *Wallace Stevens: An Anatomy of Figuration* (Philadelphia: University of Pensylvania Press, 1965), p.45.

102. In her monumental work *Mysticism: A Study in the Nature and Development of Man's Spiritual Consciousness* (New York: Dutton, 1957), p.4, Evelyn Underhill, in pointing out the mystic's

necessity for self-denial, draws also a parallel for the modern artist's own destructive/creative ways of exploring human immanence: "We must pull down our own card houses—descend, as the mystics say, `into our own nothingness'—and examine for ourselves the foundations of all possible human experience."

103. As George Steiner points out in *Language and Silence* (Harmondsworth, Middlesex: Penguin, 1969), p.31: "Our highest, purest reach of the contemplative act is that which has learned to leave language behind. The ineffable lies beyond the frontiers of the word."

104. *Selected Essays*, (New York: Random House, 1954), p.26.

105. *The Clairvoyant Eye*, p.183.

106. *Ringers in the Tower*, p.337.

107. According to William Bevis (*Mind of Winter*, p.259), "The consciousness behind Stevens' meditations, the ultimate voice of these poems, is that of the most detached observer watching the mind in the act of finding the sufficient insufficient, and vice versa." It seems to me that he confuses the outward detachment of Stevens' poetic meditations with the ceaseless creative effort required in feeding and sustaining such meditations.

CHAPTER III

Beyond Music

> A nature that is created in what it says.
> Wallace Stevens, "Things in August"

1

On account of its "spontaneous, fragmented qualities"[1] and overall complexity, it appears that Stevens' verse lends itself to easy and instructive comparison with other major art forms, particularly those of music and painting. In discussing the affinities shared by these arts, Wylie Sypher stresses the fact that they all lack what he calls "an absolute perspective" or unifying aesthetic principle, and that the intense preoccupation of modernist poetry with experimentation and impersonal technique "brings it into line with abstract painting" and atonal music.[2] Finally, with reference to Stevens' imagination, Sypher observes that it "is not a rational activity but, rather, it takes its dominance in musical form," and points out that "The great problem with Stevens, as with Kandinsky, was to know with what to replace the mere object." According to him, in the end, Stevens manages to escape from the tyranny of inert objects by turning them into "figurations of the mind,"[3] thus giving to his poetry its distinctive painterly and musical qualities. I believe that the final canto (xxxi) in "An Ordinary Evening in New Haven" provides, in this regard, the best example of a poem wherein both musical and visual effects are actively present to an equal degree:

129

A Cure of the Mind

The less legible meanings of sounds, the little reds
Not often realized, the lighter words
In the heavy drum of speech, the inner men

Behind the outer shields, the sheets of music
In the strokes of thunder, dead candles at the window
When day comes, fire-foams in the motions of the sea,

Flickings from finikin to fine finikin
And the general fidget from busts of Constantine
To photographs of the late president, Mr. Blank,

These are endings and inchings of final form,
The swarming activities of the formulae
Of statement, directly and indirectly getting at,

Like an evening evoking the spectrum of violet,
A philosopher practicing scales on his piano,
A woman writing a note and tearing it up.

It is not in the premise that reality
Is a solid. It may be a shade that traverses
A dust, a force that traverses a shade.
                    (CP 488-89)

The first impression one has in reading this poem is that of an assemblage of concrete and abstract particulars whose very dissimilarities and random juxtaposition remind us of the surface and texture of a collagist painting; and in subsequent readings of the poem what comes to mind is Eliot's description of the modernist poetic sensibility at work:

A Cure of the Mind

When a poet's mind is perfectly equipped for his work he is constantly amalgamating disparate experience; the ordinary man's experience is chaotic, irregular, fragmentary. The latter falls in love or reads Spinoza, and these two have nothing to do with each other, or with the noise of the typewriter or with the smell of cooking; in the mind of the poet these experiences are always forming new wholes. [4]

However, and notwithstanding Eliot's claim, no matter how closely one may try to read the poem, it stubbornly refuses to yield a larger `whole', so that it remains to the very end a mere "juxtaposition" of incongruous objects and random perceptions "without [a] cupola"[5] or cohering interrelatedness. Thus, reduced to purely poetic figurations, the canto's mélange of disconnected details may be legitimately compared to an action painter's own highly energized, haphazard, and disjunctive brush strokes delivered on a white canvas:

What was to go on the canvas was not a picture but an event. . .The painter no longer approached his easel with an image in his mind; he went up to it with material in his hand to do something to that other piece of material in front of him. The image would be the result of this encounter. [6]

This comes very close to describing Stevens' own metaphysician-poet who, in order to be truly inspired and write his mind poem, must work `in the dark'; but what is even more striking, is the similarity of the aesthetic urge as well as state of mind that impels both the Stevensian metaphysician-poet and an action painter to creation; thus, according to the latter, when painting a picture:

. . .anything is relevant to it. Anything that has to do with action, psychology, philosophy, history, mythology, hero worship. Anything but art criticism. The painter gets

away from art through his act of painting; the critic can't
get away from it. The critic who goes on judging in terms
of schools, styles, forms—as if the painter were still
concerned with trying to produce a certain kind of object
(the work of art), instead of living on the canvas—is
bound to seem a stranger.[7]

In the end, whatever meaning or rational coherence the canto
may be said to have, it can only be derived from its pure
resonance of sound and rhythm; an inner music that causes the
entire poem to undulate in the reader's mind from beginning to
end, and finally terminate with that exquisite last tercet whose
perceptual nuances could only be expressed in musical terms.[8]

"Montrachet-le-Jardin" constitutes a unique example of
this kind of Stevensian inner music, and its first seven tercets are
highly characteristic of the poem's complex musicality and
inaccessible tropes as a whole:[9]

What more is there to love than I have loved?
And if there be nothing more, O bright, O bright,
The chick, the chidder-barn and grassy chives

And great moon, cricket-impresario,
And, hoy, the impopulous purple-plated past,
Hoy, hoy, the blue bulls kneeling down to rest.

Chome! clicks the clock, if there be nothing more.
But if, but if there be something more to love,
Something in now a senseless syllable,

A shadow in the mind, a flourisher
Of sounds resembling sounds, efflorisant,
Approaching the feelings or come down from them,
These other shadows, not in the mind, players
Of aphonies, tuned in from zero and

A Cure of the Mind

Beyond, futura's fuddle-fiddling lumps,

But if there be something more to love, amen,
Amen to the feelings about familiar things,
The blessed regal dropped in daggers' dew,

Amen to thought, our singular skeleton,
Salt-flicker, amen to our accustomed cell,
The moonlight in the cell, words on the wall.
(*CP* 260)

Whatever the poem's intended or ultimate meaning might be, it is quite evident that given the structure and flow of Stevens' language it can only be reached by tuning in to his subtle modalities of thought and feeling as orchestrated in words; which is to say, we must free our mind of all ratiocination so as to become totally open and receptive to Stevens' spell-binding evocations of sound and trope; thus, we would be able to identify the true significance that his highly volatized verses may be said to have for us. Be that as it may, "Montrachet-le-Jardin" is the type of poem which, according to Riddel, is "a series of poetic asides jotted down for one's ears";[10] and in such a way that the mind cannot detect the slightest thematic clue. This is due to the mind's entanglement in the poem's "bewildering series of transitions" which, with each successive tercet, begin to "reflect the endless and surprising quality of an absolutely open consciousness."[11] In short, reading this very Stevensian poem is very similar to the experience of listening to a highly variational piece of modern music, whose effect on the mind is as jarringly disjunctive as it is, in other instances, perfectly harmonious and fluid.[12] Finally, what is remarkable about the poem is its appropriate ending or denouement; a fitting finale which, as is also the case with canto xxxi in "An Ordinary Evening in New

133

Haven," strongly underscores Stevens' perspectivist view of reality and his obsessive need to capture its evanescence in words:

> *And yet what good were yesterday's devotions?*
> *I affirm and then at midnight the great cat*
> *Leaps quickly from the fireside and is gone.* (CP 264)

"Montrachet-le-Jardin" is a prime example of Stevens' conception of poetry as an act of the mind, hence its complexity.[13] It is the kind of poem Stevens liked to write in order to experience the profound effect its inner music had on his mind. Thus, the indeterminable musicality and thematic diffuseness of Stevens' mind poems not only testify to his open poetic consciousness, but also sustain it as a vital precondition for the writing of such poetry. What needs to be established now is the method and extent to which Stevens' mind revitalizes itself by its own music.

2

What needs to be made clear at the very outset is that the kind of music Stevens' verse generates does not have its roots in Symbolist poetics, whose primary aim is to create an ideal reality sustained by constant invocations to "sterility, purity, and beauty";[14] on the contrary, Stevens' own powerful and haunting music reflects a strong ontological urge that finds its true resonance in the "subverbal sounds"[15] of his creative subconscious. What this means in poetic terms is that his harmonies are not the result of a conscious manipulation of words, as is the case with the Symbolists' systematic musicalization of language; rather, in Stevens' case, music is an intrinsic quality of his mind, grown out of his intense and constantly changing response to life and self. Thus, its complex modalities become accessible and penetrable only when seen and heard as the result of strong imaginative troping, accruing from the ceaseless and dynamic interplay of `mind and sensibility.'[16] And what impels Stevens to such "an innate music" (*CP* 277) is a strongly felt fidelity to the authentic sources of his own poetic voice: "I am myself part of what is real, and it is my own speech and the strength of it, this only, that I hear or ever shall" (*NA* 60). Therefore, according to him, the only music poetry should aim at is that which is created "for internal reasons and not with reference to an external program" (*L* 438).

Had Stevens chosen to create the kind of unreal self-music[17] that the Symbolists pursued, he would have had to totally privatize all his experiences of self and world; and had he indeed decided to do so, he would then have had to turn the poetic act into something that reduces, whatever is vital in life and thought, into sheer poetic essence. In short, he would have done what Mallarmé did, who, on account of his excesses of style and language, ended up with a poetic idiom so refined and precious that it eventually musicalized itself itno a state of acute aesthetic anemia from which it never recovered. However, Stevens spared himself a similar fate by the judicious choice of allowing his conscious mind and free imagination to become involved in a lifelong and vital dialogic play that made them both creatively interdependent and closely attuned to each other:[18]

> *The self*
> *Detects the sound of a voice that doubles its own,*
> *In the images of desire, the forms that speak,*
> *The ideas that come to it with a sense of speech.* (*OP* 82)

And this dialogic relationship between the conscious mind and the creative imagination is troped into a listening inner `ear'; and as is the case with Stevens' `eye'—that which radically transforms sight into vision,[19]—it too is an ear that converts all the sounds it receives into interior music:

A Cure of the Mind

> *The flight of eye and ear, the highest eye*
> *And the lowest ear, the deep ear that discerns,*
> *At evenings, things that attend it* until it hears
> The supernatural preludes of its own. . .[20]
> (CP 414; emphasis mine)

And:

> *Now, closely the ear attends the varying*
> *Of this precarious music, the change of key*
>
> *Not quite detected at the moment of change*
> *And, now, it attends the difficult difference.* (CP 332)

This dialogic aspect of Stevens' poetic mind is given its earliest expression in "Sunday Morning" (1915), and it is enacted in the ongoing conversation between the poet and his female persona: the lady who, sitting "in a sunny chair' lamenting the death of the great Christian metaphysic, feels "The need of some imperishable bliss" (CP 66,68). And six years later, in his short lyric "Tea at the Palaz of Hoon" (1921), Stevens openly celebrates with great depth of feeling and exultant joy the prodigious powers of his imagination:

> *What was the ointment sprinkles on my beard?*
> *What were* the hymns that buzzed beside my ears?
> *What was the sea whose tide swept through me there?*
>
> *Out of my mind the golden ointment rained,*
> And my ears made the blowing hymns they heard.
> *I was myself the compass of that sea.*
> (CP 65; emphasis mine)

The key line here is `my ears made the blowing hymns they heard', and the meaning that it conveys is unequivocal: authentic music does not reside in the manipulation of words or empty sounds, but in our innermost modalities of image, thought, and feeling; that is, in

> *transparencies of sound,*
> *Sounding in transparent dwellings of the self;* (CP 466)

or, in

> *Sounds passing through sudden rightness,* wholly
> Containing the mind. (*CP* 240; emphasis mine)

But it is "Of Modern Poetry" (1940) that makes us fully aware of the extent to which Stevens' imagination is dependent on this dialogic element as a source of creative sustenance; self-dialogue is now posited not only as the indispensable basis for the poetry of the mind, but it is also given the status of what sounds like a poetic manifesto:

> *It has*
> *To construct a new stage. It has to be on that stage*
> *And, like an insatiable actor, slowly and*
> *With meditation,* speak words that in the ear,
> In the delicatest ear of the mind, repeat,
> Exactly, that which it wants to hear, *at the sound*
> *Of which, an invisible audience listens,*
> *Not to the play, but to itself, expressed*
> *In an emotion as of two people,* as of two
> Emotions becoming one. (*CP* 240; emphasis mine)

What we have here is an extended trope, or, more accurately, three tropes in one: firstly, we have the poem of the mind entrusted with the task of constructing `a new stage'; secondly, we have the `ear' as a trope for the inner poetic mind—the `spirit's alchemicana' that creates and listens ('in the dark') to "its floraisons of imagery" and "majesties of sound"[21] (*OP* 47, *CP* 125); and thirdly, we have the two dialogic halves of Stevens' poetic self troped as `two emotions becoming one'. One could also persuasively argue that the entire passage is a trope that addresses itself to the interior process by which Stevens' mind converts a poem into a piece of verbal music wherein it finally finds its true transcendence and cure. And the apotheosis of this conception of poetry as an inner dialogic process, finds its fullest expression in canto xi of "Chocorua to Its Neighbor" (1943):

> *My solitaria*
> *Are the meditations of a central mind.*
> *I hear the motions of the spirit and the sound*
> *Of what is secret becomes, for me,* a voice
> That is my own voice speaking in my ear.
> (*CP* 298; emphasis mine)

As the canto makes clear, `solitaria' refers to Stevens' meditations—the `motions of the spirit'—which eventually orchestrate themselves through figuration and trope into the kind of inner music he is so ardently intent on achieving; however, the exquisite inwardness of this music is such that it eventually makes itself totally self-sealed and distant from the realm of ordinary human experience.[22]

Nevertheless, this is the kind of music that feeds Stevens' mind and soul, and therefore he abides by it. Eliot gives us an eloquent and precise account of what kind of poetic music it is:

> *to write poetry which should be essentially poetry, with nothing poetic about it, poetry standing naked in its bare bones, or poetry so transparent that we should not see the poetry. . .that in reading it we are intent on what the poem points at, and not on the poetry, this seems to me the thing to try for. To get* beyond poetry, *as Beethoven, in*

his later works, strove to get beyond music (Eliot's emphasis).[23]

It is truly remarkable, given their radical differences in temperament, sensibility, and approach to poetry, how closely affined Stevens' own conception of poetic music is to that of Eliot's:

> *It is suddenly to believe in the poem as one has never believed in it before, suddenly to require of it a meaning beyond what its words can possibly say, a sound beyond any giving of the ear, a motion beyond our previous knowledge of feeling (OP 210).*

It becomes increasingly obvious then—and this applies to Eliot as well—that what Stevens strives to attain by such precious inner music is a state of mind that goes beyond the scope or bounds of ordinary poetic discourse; a transcendent apperception of self and world[24] that has as its *locus classicus* canto x, Part II, of "Notes toward a Supreme Fiction":

> *A bench was his catalepsy, Theatre*
> *of Trope. He sat in the park. The water of*
> *The lake was full of artificial things,*
>
> *Like a page of music, like an upper air,*
> *Like a momentary color, in which swans*
> *Were seraphs, were saints, were changing essences.*
>
> *The west wind was the music, the motion, the force*
> *To which swans curveted, a will to change,*
> *A will to make iris frettings on the blank.* (CP 397)

Catalepsy, in the sense which Stevens uses the word here, is the culmination and true meaning of his conception of poetry as an act of the mind; a poetry whose ultimate aim is to attain the kind of inner music that would give him, however momentarily, that unity of being and equanimity that he craves so much both as man and poet;[25] in short, a music that for him resides in

> *the sound*
> *Of right joining, a music of ideas, the burning*
> *And breeding and bearing birth of harmony,*
> *The final relation, the marriage of the rest.* (CP 464-65)

It seems then, that by writing a verse whose "perfection [and] unalterable vibration" (*NA* 32) echoes the deepest recesses of being, Stevens was able, for a miraculous moment, to become the music that his words had created.

3

Whatever its deeper psychic reverberations might be, music in verse is eventually created by the inherent power and appeal of words;[26] and in Stevens' case it is attained by the intricate tropes and figurations of his poetry of mind, which as such is governed almost exclusively by what Mallarmé calls "the demon of infinite analogy."[27] It is my belief that the most unobstrusive way to approach or try and fathom Stevens' complex use of metaphors[28] is to proceed on the following premise: (a) that his metaphors do not seek to enhance and thus reaffirm the essential integrity or quiddity of things;[29] and (b) that in fact their only aim is to reassert the supremacy of the imagination over `things as they are', and in so doing allow the mind to occasionally experience the kind of ontological renewal it so keenly craves for.[30] In "Three Academic Pieces," his major text on what he calls analogy and resemblance, Stevens expounds at some length on his theory of metaphor:

> *The study of the activity of resemblance is an approach to the understanding of poetry. Poetry is a satisfying of the desire for resemblance. As the mere satisfying of a desire, it*

140

is pleasurable. But poetry if it did nothing but satisfy a desire would not rise above the level of many lesser things. Its singularity is that in the act of satisfying the desire for resemblance it touches the sense of reality, it enhances the sense of reality, heightens it, intensifies it. If resemblance is described as a partial similarity between two dissimilar things, it complements and reinforces that which the two dissimilar things have in common. It makes it brilliant. When the similarity is between things of adequate dignity, the resemblance may be said to transfigure or to sublimate them. . .In this ambiguity, the intensification of reality by resemblance increases realization and this increased realization is pleasurable. It is as if a man who lived indoors should go outdoors on a day of sympathetic weather. His realization of the weather would exceed that of a man who lives outdoors. It might, in fact, be intense enough to convert the real world about him into an imagined world. In short, a sense of reality keen enough to be in excess of the normal sense of reality creates a reality of its own. Here what matters is that the intensification of the sense of reality creates a resemblance: that reality of its own is a reality. (NA 77,79)

Although he initially accepts the idea that a metaphor `reinforces that which two dissimilar things have in common', at the end of his discourse Stevens openly admits that the true essence of metaphorical language lies in the fact that it `creates a reality of its own'; as he characteristically puts it in one of his adagia: "Metaphor creates a new reality in which the original appears unreal" (OP 169). Thus, for Stevens, metaphors not only become "an integral ingredient of his poetry,"[31] but also "a transcendent analogue composed of the particulars of reality"; and as such, they create for him "a world that transcends the world and a life livable in that transcendence" (*NA* 130). As he says elsewhere in "Three Academic Pieces," "What our eyes behold may well be the text of life but one's meditations on the text and the disclosures of these meditations are no less a part of the structure of reality" (*NA* 76). For Stevens then, metaphors not only empower the mind to impose order on the chaotic flux of outer reality,[32] but also allow the self to momentarily recapture its inner unity by converting, through the metaphoric play of mind and sensibility, inert objects into "creations of being."[33] As Hillis Miller perceptively observes, metaphors become "the most powerful instrument of the perspectivist poet" in that they help him "sublimate(s)" his "apprehension of things."[34]

Stevens further expounds his views on metaphor in what one might call four theoretical poems, namely: "Poem Written at Morning," "The Motive for Metaphor," "Description without Place," and "Metaphor as Degeneration." His conception of metaphor, as stated in the first three stanzas of "Poem Written at Morning," is unequivocally clear:

> *A sunny day's complete Poussiniana*
> *Divide it from itself. It is this or that*
> *And it is not.*
> *By metaphor you paint*
> *A thing. Thus, the pineapple was a leather fruit,*
> *A fruit for pewter, thorned and palmed and blue,*
> *To be served by men of ice.*
> *The senses paint*
> *By metaphor. The juice was fragranter*
> *Than wettest cinnamon. It was cribled pears*
> *Dripping a morning sap.* (CP 219)

As morning progresses and its hues change with the changing sunlight, the mind turns into a riot of fickle impressions and the day becomes divided—'It is this or that/And it is not'. On the other hand, when the mind paints a thing, it not only turns it into an aesthetic artifact but also enhances its primary qualities, so that things become `cribled pears/Dripping a morning sap'. There is, however, an underlying irony: the creative profusions of the metaphorical mind are as fickle and unpredictable as the morning sunlight itself: "The resources of the imagination's Poussiniana are apparently endless, and no one image can suffice to paint a thing."[35] Also, in the appropriately entitled poem "The Motive for Metaphor," Stevens stresses what I would call the quasi-ontological aspect of metaphor, that is, its more than strictly aesthetic effect on the mind:

> You like it under the trees in autumn,
> Because everything is half dead.
> The wind moves like a cripple among the leaves
> And repeats words without meaning.
>
> In the same way, you were happy in spring,
> With the half colors of quarter-things,
> The slightly brighter sky, the melting clouds,
> The single bird, the obscure moon—
>
> The obscure moon lighting an obscure world
> Of things that would never be quite expressed,
> Where you yourself were never quite yourself
> And did not want nor have to be,
>
> Desiring the exhilarations of changes:
> The motive for metaphor, shrinking from
> The weight of primary noon,
> The A B C of being.

A Cure of the Mind

The ruddy temper, the hammer
Of red and blue, the hard sound—
Steel against intimation—the sharp flash,
The vital, arrogant, fatal, dominant X. (CP 288)

At the beginning of the poem Stevens intimates how innately metaphoric his imagination is: it is much taken `With the half colors of quarter-things in spring', and likes `it under the trees in autumn' because `The wind moves like a cripple among the leaves/And repeats words without meaning'. What we have here, once again, is a strong identification between the random changes in the physical universe and those (meaningless?) `floraisons' that the mind constantly undergoes. But the poem's real thematic punch is delivered in the final two stanzas: what our new metaphors finally give us is not the perceptual deadweight of spent perceptions but the healing freshness of new insights into self and world; not the predictable `A B C of being', but the creative exhilaration that comes with each fresh metaphor—'the sharp flash/The vital, arrogant, fatal, dominant X; and which `X' stands for the creative release that Stevens experiences through the proliferation of metaphors.

But the real thrust of Stevens' radical conception of metaphor is voiced in cantos v-vi of "Description without Place" which, by critical consensus, is the most abstruse of Stevens' poetic manifestos in verse:

Description is
Composed of a sight indifferent to the eye.

It is an expectation, a desire,
A palm that rises up beyond the sea,

A little different from reality:
....

144

A Cure of the Mind

Description is revelation. It is not
The thing described, nor false facsimile.

It is an artificial thing that exists,
In its own seeming, plainly visible,

Yet not too closely the double of our lives,
Intenser than any actual life could be,

A text we should be born that we might read,
More explicit than the experience of sun. (CP 343-44)

What Stevens openly confesses here is his impelling need to use
metaphors not simply as a way of capturing the true essence of
things, but actually as *a means of creating such an essence by
perceptually transforming them*; so that for him true description is
an act of pure poetic invention, not an objective documentation
of the physical contour of things. So employed, what metaphors
finally create is something which, although `intenser than any
actual life could be', in the end remains `an artificial thing that
exists in its own seeming'. Thus, the true import of these lines is
that they accentuate Stevens' ambivalence concerning the power
of metaphors to effect the sought-for integration of self and
world. In what is the most comprehensible passage in the entire
poem, sustained by a powerful modulation of thought and
feeling, Stevens voices this ambivalence with great resonance:

There might be, too, a change immenser than
A poet's metaphors in which being would

Come true, a point in the fire of music where
Dazzle yields to a clarity and we observe,

And observing is completing and we are content,
In a world that shrinks to an immediate whole,

That we do not need to understand, complete
Without secret arrangements of it in the mind. (CP 341)

Finally, in the opening canto of "Someone Puts a Pineapple Together" Stevens proceeds to describe, or `put together', a pineapple; not, however, by enhancing and thus reaffirming its inviolate immanence, but by reducing it through metaphoric twists of language to a series of totally unreal figurations:[36]

O juventes, O filii, he contemplates
A wholly artificial nature, in which
The profusion of metaphor has been increased.

It is something on a table that he sees,
The root of a form, as of this fruit, a fund,
The angel at the centre of this rind,

This husk of Cuba, tufted emerald,
Himself, may be, the irreducible X
At the bottom of imagined artifice,

Its inhabitant and elect expositor.
It is as if there were three planets: the sun,
The moon and the imagination, or, say,

Day, night and man and his endless effigies.
If he sees an object on a table, much like
A jar of the shoots of an infant country, green

And bright, or like a venerable urn,
Which, from the ash within it, fortifies

A Cure of the Mind

A green that is the ash of what green is,

He sees it in the tangent of himself.
And in this tangent it becomes a thing
Of weight, on which the weightless rests. (PM 295-96)

And in canto ii he gives us, in equally unreal figurations, his
theory of metaphor as applied to the poem as a whole:

He must say nothing of the fruit that is
Not true, nor think it, less. He must defy
The metaphor that murders metaphor.

He seeks as image a second of the self,
Made subtle by truth's most jealous subtlety,
Like the true light of the truest sun, the true

Power in the waving of the wand of the moon,
Whose shining is the intelligence of our sleep.
He seeks an image certain as meaning is

To sound, sound's substance and executant,
The particular tingle in a proclamation
That makes it say the little thing it says,

Below the prerogative jumble. The fruit so seen
As a part of the nature that he contemplates
Is fertile with more than changes of the light.

On the table or in the colors of the room.
Its propagations are more erudite,
Like precious scholia jotted in the dark.

Did not the age that bore him bear him among

A Cure of the Mind

Its infiltrations? There had been an age
When a pineapple on the table was enough,

Without the forfeit scholar coming in,
Without his enlargings and pale arrondissements,
Without the furious roar in his capital. (PM 296-97)

What Stevens chooses to see in `the fruit that he contemplates'
is a thing `fertile with more than the changes of the light'; in
fact, his contemplation is so penetrating and intense that the
fruit finally becomes "the sum of its complications, seen/And
Unseen": a "total artifice [that] reveals itself/As the total reality"
(*PM* 299). What this means is that the pineapple in question is
eventually reduced to a series of highly unlikely or abstruse
figurations,[36] which literally savage the fruit's physical integrity
by turning it into a purely verbal construct; in fact to such an
extreme degree that it finally becomes in Stevens' mind an
"irreducible X/At the bottom of imagined artifice" (*PM* 295). In
the end, what this relentless metaphorizing proves is only one
thing: that the poem constitutes the very apotheosis of Stevens'
poetry of mind as an act of finding `what will suffice'; and as
such, it allows us to have an inside view of the way the spirit's
alchemicana performs to maximum effect; except that the
alchemy in this particular case is the reduction of a material
object to a series of abstract poetic figurations—an act which,
once again, permits the mind to renew itself ontologically.[37] I
think this interpretation is validated by what I consider to be the
one crucial image in the entire poem: that of the `scholar' who is
given to the task of `jotting down' his `precious scholia' in the
dark. Needless to say, the scholar alluded to here is a variant of
Stevens' other two similar personas already encountered in "The
Man with the Blue Guitar" and "Of Modern Poetry," since all
three are closely related by the fact that they are engaged in an

148

identical act: that of writing a mind poem `in the dark'. The only difference in the pineapple poem is that here Stevens' allusion to the workings of `mind and sensibility' or `poem of the mind' is much more direct, referring to both of them as `scholia', which is of course a trope for his poetic metaphors, what he calls "erudite propagations" and "molten mixings" (*PM* 297,299).

As I have already argued, Stevens' excessive use of figurative language—exemplified to an extreme degree in "Someone Puts a Pineapple Together"—is instrumental in augmenting the kind of self-mystification or inner-music through which he undergoes a profound reintegration of self and world.[38] However, the reduction of poetic speech to pure metaphor, whereby things become totally denatured or divorced from their living immanence, perforce brings poetry to the verge of the irrational; and yet, Stevens not only allows himself to come to the very brink of irrationality, but is prepared at all times to take a leap even into total incomprehension. I believe that he is willing to do so because his creative instinct tells him that "logical thought is far inferior to the pre-logical mind because the latter is `deeper' and comes from farther away";[39] therefore, he feels impelled to give himself to "the contemplation of the world independently of the principle of reason."[40] As he himself puts it in his own aphoristic way, "Life's nonsense pierces us with strange relation" (*CP* 383). Thus, according to him, a true poet not only affirms "the efficacy of the irrational" (*OP* 228) as a vital source of poetic renewal, but also "finds joy in [it]" (*OP* 229).[41] The supreme irony in all of this, however, is the fact that Stevens, in undertaking to celebrate `life's nonsense' must, like the true perspectivist that he is, do so by involving himself with the even vaster irrational interiorities of perception, word, and sound. And this is conclusively evinced by his' poetic performance in "Someone Puts a Pineapple Together," where his metaphors do "hypostatize resemblance into an autonomous entity."[42] And it is this irrational use of language that makes Stevens openly admit that "Metaphor creates a new reality from which the original appears to be unreal" (*OP* 169).

4

It was Nietzsche who first detected and pointed out the subversive nature of metaphors; that is, their power to undermine and finally break down the rigid categories of rational thought:

> *The drive toward the formation of metaphors is the fundamental human drive, which one cannot for a single instant dispense with in thought, for one would thereby dispense with man himself. . .This drive* continually confuses the conceptual categories *and cells by bringing forward new transferences, metaphors, and metonymies. It continually manifests an ardent desire to refashion the world which presents itself to waking man,* so that it will be colorful, irregular, lacking in results and coherence, *charming, and eternally new as the world of dreams* (emphasis mine).[43]

The main implication of Nietzche's argument is that the creative uses of metaphorical thinking in art provide a much more vital and meaningful alternative to the logical categorizations of human experience:

> *Aesthetic experience is incomparably richer* [than sense perception]. *It is pregnant with infinite possibilities which remain unrealized in ordinary sense experience. In the work of the artist these possibilities become actualities, they are brough into the open and take on a definite shape. The revelation of this inexhaustibility of the aspects of*

things is one of the great privileges and one of the deepest charms of art.[44]

But the second and more far-reaching implication underlying Nietzche's argument is that metaphors are directly involved in fomenting and promoting the irrational as the most creative and indispensable element in art.[45] In fact, since the Romantics, "the powers of unreason" are the only venue modern man has for reaching "infinity,"[46] or taking himself "out of this world";[47] so that, in Yeats' famous pronouncement, "the irrational cry" has become our "last surrender [and] revelation—the scream of Juno's peacock."[48] Jacques Maritain offers what is perhaps the most persuasive and eloquent rationale for the uses of the irrational in art, particularly in modern poetry:

Rational language is not cut out to express the singular, it is burdened with social and utilitarian connotations, ready-made associations, and worn-out meanings, it is invaded by the inevitable insipidity which results from habit. . .Why should we be surprised by the fact that modern artists struggle to free themselves from rational language and its logical laws? Never did they pay more attention to words, never did they attach greater importance to words: but in order to transfigure them, and to get clear of the language of discursive reason. Joyce creates with all the words of the earth a new language conveying an intelligible sense, but intelligible to himself alone. . .Is it true that the logical sense has disappeared? No, that's impossible. But the logical sense has been digested, so to speak, by the poetic sense, it has been broken up, dislocated, to subsist only as a kind of variegated matter of the poetic sense. The poetic sense alone gleams in the dark. This poetic sense, which is but one with poetry itself, is the inner, ontologic entelechy of the poem, and gives it its very being and substantial significance. It is in no way identical with the intelligible sense, as the soul of a man is in no way identical with his speech; and it is inseparable from the formal structure of the poetic work: whether the work is clear or obscure, the poetic sense is there, whatever becomes of the intelligible sense. The poetic sense is substantially bound to the form, immanent in the organism of words, immanent in the poetic structure as a whole. In modern art it demands to be definitively freed, at any cost.[49]

And Marcel Raymond further expounds, in more specific terms, on the true origin and nature of the irrational impulse in modern poetry as follows:

In the world that man has built for his use, where he feels at home, in safety, protected by reason, morality, society, the police, sheltered in cities where the birds of the sky can no longer be seen, in houses, in rooms, in "comfortable" ideas, with the pleasant possibility of roaming a bit along the beaten paths that he calls his freedom, surrounded by conventions which he regards as necessary truths—in this fictitious world that is thought to be real, on this planet hurled into space (but no one suspects it!), a poet makes his appearance. At first it will be difficult for him to be anything other than a sower of disturbances, an instigator of disorder. His primary mission is to disorientate. Gradually he will reveal the original meaninglessness of the world. . .when an industrial civilization is dreaming of subjecting the mind to the rigorous laws that prevail in physics, the poet's task will be to unsettle man, to make him lose heart in the face of his life and the world, and to put him in permanent contact with the irrational.[50]

Therefore, "the [modern] poet's gift of spontaneously feeling things" is not motivated by "their logical relationships," but by "their essence and the spiritual analogies revealed to the imagination." Thus, according to Raymond, what the modern poet creates is,

> . . .*a poetry of fulgurant marvels, brief touches, phantom-images, poetic islets on the blank page, light as foam, as distinct from language as a divene voice be from all the noise of the earth. It has been called a poetry of the eternal present, whose source begins at the point where man's inner being, having eradicated the stigmata of the individual, adheres to the present which concentrates in its depths all the depths of life.*[51]

Stevens' own espousal of the irrational constitutes an integral and highly significant part of both his theory and practice of poetry. Once, in offering to Samuel French Morse a gloss for "The Emperor of Ice-Cream," he made what appears to be a case for the use of the irrational in his own verse:

> *Things that have their origin in the imagination or in the emotions (poems) very often have meanings that differ in nature from the meanings of things that have their origin in reason. They have imaginative or emotional meanings, not rational meanings, and they communicate these meanings to people who are susceptible to imaginative or emotional meanings. They may communicate nothing at all to people who are open only to rational meanings.*[52]

In the course of the same conversation, Stevens went on to say that "one never knows what prompts an artist to do what he does," and that he himself "did not know what he was doing when he wrote a poem," a fact that made him have "respect for the fortuitousness of the poetic impulse."[53] As Stevens confesses elsewhere: "It is not possible to tell what one's own poems mean, or were intended to mean, [and that] as soon as I start to rationalize, I lose the poetry of the idea." (*L* 354,435).

In Stevens' case then, the irrational may be defined as the illogical image or trope that accrues from the purely fortuitous conjunction of thought and feeling spontaneously expressed; and this definition is adumbrated in the final stanza of "Poem Written at Morning":

The truth must be
That you do not see, you experience, you feel,
That the buxom eye brings merely its element

To the total thing, a shapeless giant forced
Upward.
Green were the curls upon the head. (CP 219)

What Stevens reaffirms in this stanza is the `reality of the other eye,' a theory of perception he deals with at greater length in "Description without Place" and "The Bouquet," which I have already discussed in a different context. Stevens' emphasis here is specifically on the irrational aspect of poetic creation; thus, he strongly urges his creative self not `merely' to `see' but to `experience' and to `feel'; and this urge stems from his belief that `truth' is not to be found in `the buxom eye,' that is, in what our eye observes, but in what Stevens calls `the total thing'. And what this crucial phrase refers to is the perceptual range, inner coherence, and depth of Stevens' irrational poetic intuitions: irrational in the sense that they are totally divorced from the living realities of self and world, and that they derive their imaginative strength and viability from the profound, integrative effect they have on Stevens' own mind. As for the final line in the stanza—'green were the curls upon that head'—it is paradigmatic of the theory Stevens propounds in the poem as a whole, which is the poetic use of the illogical image or trope in verse. Finally, with reference to the `shapeless giant' alluded to in the stanza, it is a trope that addresses itself to the irrational and inconstant nature of man's creative endevors, a theme Stevens deals with at greater depth in "A Primitive Like an Orb."

A Cure of the Mind

In this poem the giant is given a semi-human shape and is presented as an "angelic" and "plenteous" being who "Imposes power by the power of his form."[54] (*CP* 443) Doubtlessly, as conceived and projected in the poem, he is a symbolic embodiment of the irrational impulses that govern all of man's creations, be they of heart, mind, or spirit:

> *That's it. The lover writes, the believer hears,*
> *The poet mumbles and the painter sees,*
> *Each one his fated eccentricity,*
> *As a part, but part, but tenacious particle,*
> *Of the skeleton of the ether, the total*
> *Of letters, prophecies, perceptions, clods*
> *Of color, the giant of nothingness, each one*
> *And the giant ever changing, living in change.* (*CP* 443)

But it is in "The Creations of Sound" that Stevens makes what is his strongest and most impassioned case for the use of the irrational in poetry:

> *If the poetry of X was music,*
> *So that it came to him of its own,*
> *Without understanding, out of the wall*
>
> *Or in the ceiling, in sounds not chosen,*
> *Or chosen quickly, in a freedom*
> *That was their element, we should not know*
>
> *That X is an obstruction, a man*
> *Too exactly himself, and that there are words*
> *Better without an author, without a poet,*
>
> *Or having a separate author, a different poet,*
> *An accretion from ourselves, intelligent*
> *Beyond intelligence, an artificial man*

A Cure of the Mind

At a distance, a secondary expositor,
A being of sound, whom one does not approach
Through any exaggeration. From him, we collect.

Tell X that speech is not dirty silence
Clarified. It is silence made still dirtier.
It is more than an imitation for the ear.

He lacks this venerable complication.
His poems are not of the second part of life.
They do not make the visible a little hard

To see nor, reverberating, eke out the mind
On peculiar horns, themselves eked out
By the spontaneous particulars of sound.

We do not say ourselves like that in poems.
We say ourvelves in syllables that rise
From the floor, rising in speech we do not speak.
             (CP 310-11)

What Stevens openly advocates in the poem[55] is a verse whose music should come `of its own', and `in sounds not chosen, or chosen quickly, in a freedom that was their element'; and furthermore, the poet who writes such verse ought to be `a being of sound' who makes `the visible a little hard to see'. Needless to say, what Stevens asserts here is his conception of poetry as an act of mind, stressing in particular the inner workings of the spirit's alchemicana that take place `in the dark'. Thus the speech that eventually emerges from such an intensely rarefied poetry `is more than an imitation for the ear': it is a speech which, born of the `spontaneous particulars of sound,' we can only `say in syllables that rise from the floor.'[56] What Stevens wishes to underscore by this last image are not only the inscrutable workings of the poetic subconscious, but also the fact that illogically conceived tropes or metaphors can surface, almost intact, in our conscious, `literate' mind. In three amusingly bizarre tercets, in "Notes toward a Supreme Fiction," he dramatizes for us how the poetic imagination engenders the irrational and puts it to its own uses:

> *We say: At night an Arabian in my room,*
> *With his damned hoobla-hoobla-hoobla-how,*
> *Inscribes a primitive astronomy*
>
> *Across the unscrawled fores the future casts*
> *And throws his stars around the floor. By day*
> *The wood-dove used to chant his hoobla-hoo*
>
> *And still the grossest iridescence of ocean*
> *Howls hoo and rises and howls hoo and falls.*
> *Life's nonsense pierces us with strange relation.* (CP 383)

The theory Stevens propounds in these verses is quite clear: what we consider to be the irrational element in poetry accrues from the fortuitous conception of illogical images or tropes which the poet voices without any inhibition or self-restraint. As he put it once to Samuel French Morse, for him "the meaning of a particular poem" is inseperable from the impulse that made him "set down the first thing that came into his head."[57]

In concluding, we can say that Stevens' metaphors must be seen for what they really are: mere appendages to the poem as an act of the mind; that is, simply a means for augmenting and promoting the kind of self-music to which his poetic sensibility is steadfastly attuned to; and in this capacity they constitute the most irrational element of his verse:

> *There is no coherent pattern of symbols and metaphors, each one referring to all the others. One metaphor or symbol is introduced, developed for a while, then dropped.*[58]

And since they make constant use of the irrational in a creative way, Stevens' metaphors revitalize his perceptions and thus help him maintain the imaginative power and originality of his verse:

> *To resist the intelligence is, in Stevens' view, to preserve the potency of poetry, to maintain an interest in it as art against the destructive tendency of the intellect to reduce it to statement. . .It is only in the language and structure of the poem itself, impervious to the critics' doctrines, that the poet's triumph exists.*[59]

The price, however, for the kind of music Stevens so assiduously pursues by courting the irrational, in the end proves to be quite high; since, according to Valery, it is a process which ultimately results in "the complete negation of language."[60]

NOTES

1. Bevis, *Mind of Winter*, p.263.

2. *Rococo to Cubism*, pp.287,317.

3. Ibid., pp.318, 319.

4. *Selected Prose*, p.64.

5. Donald Davie, *Pound* (London: Fontana Books, 1975), p.75. Davie's phrase addresses itself to collage, fragmentation, and

parataxis, a poetic technique that interrelates Pound's and Stevens' verse much more closely than Marjorie Perloff would have us believe. In her comparison of the two poets (which is to prove that Stevens is an old-fashioned Symbolist), she commits the unpardonable sin of selecting such passages from Stevens' work (as, for example, canto v, Part III, in *Notes*) that best support her thesis. See "Pound/Stevens: Whose Era?" *The Dance of the Intellect*, pp.1-32.

6. Harold Rosenberg quoted in Spender, *Struggle of the Modern*, pp.202-203. It is interesting to note that John Ashbury (Stevens' closest epigone) also considers his poems to be "much like the `action paintings' of Jackson Pollock" (Ruland and Bradbury, *From Puritanism to Postmodernism*, p.342). However, it was Matthew Josephson who first pointed out, in his review of *Harmonium* in 1923, that Stevens' poetry "has the geometrical interest of a piece of modern abstract painting." See "An Extraordinary Personality," in *The Critical Heritage*, ed. Doyle, p.42.

7. Spender, *Struggle of the Modern*, p.204. According to Rosenberg, the essence of abstract expressionism lies in the belief that a painting "is not a picture of a thing; it's the thing itself" (Ibid., p.203). What is truly remarkable is that also, for Stevens, a poem is "Part of the res itself and not about it" (*CP* 473).

8. The canto's final tercet not only provides a telling poetic gloss for Stevens' perspectivist view of reality, but is also a verse paraphrase of Alfred North Whitehead's conceptual formulation of such a reality: "Everything is everywhere at all times, for every location involves an aspect of itself in every other location. Thus every spatio-temporal standpoint mirrors the world" (*OP* 192).

9. For a discussion of Stevens' obscure tropes and language in general, see Miller, "Theoretical and Atheoretical in Stevens," *passim*.

A Cure of the Mind

10. *The Clairvoyant Eye*, p.160.

11. Bevis, *Mind of Winter*, pp.276,277. Also, in comparing Beethoven's disjunctions to those of Emerson's prose and Stevens' longer poems, Bevis refers to the "uniquely open structure" of their later work which, according to him, manages to accommodate "transitional fragments. . .within a traditional framework" (Ibid, p.279).

12. In comparing Stevens' poetic improvizations to those of modern jazz, Bevis supports his argument by referring to Dick Katz's description of Art Tatum's piano technique (Ibid, p.276): "Tatum embarks on a harmonic flight that breaks at the very limits of the key center (G major). To these ears, it sounds as though he states the first part of a sequential phrase, and then completes it a half step higher or lower, as the case may be. However, these transitions (they aren't long enough to be termed modulations) are done with substitute, altered chord changes that create an effect of suspended animation of musical weightlessness."

13. Unable to fathom or appreciate the true modalities of the poem, Riddel refers to "Montrachet-le-Jardin" as "a practice poem" (*The Clairvoyant Eye*, p.160). On the other hand, Helen Vendler, far more sensitive and appreciative of Stevens' poetry of the mind, is able to see in the poem the true significance of his "supralogical rhymes" and "expertise in presenting several images at the same time," as well as "the necessity of improvization" and his "dazzling manipulation of objects in action" (*Extended Wings*, pp.189,194,175,193).

14. Stéphane Mallarmé, *Selected Prose Poems, Essays and Letters*, ed. Bradford Cook (Baltimore, Md.: Johns Hopkins University Press, 1956), p. 155.

15. Richard Ellman, *a long the riverrun: Selected Essays* (Harmondsworth, Middlesex: Penguin, 1989), p.234.

16. This is how Du-Hyoung Kang sums up his argument in comparing Stevens' poetics to that of the Symbolists: "Stevens is not a Symbolist. Despite many surface similarities, Stevens' theory of poetic composition differs substansively from that of the Symbolists because it abandons the quest for an absolute principle in the universe in favor of a method by which changes in reality can be incorporated into the poetic mind." See "Stasis and Continuity: Mallarmé and Wallace Stevens," *The Wallace Stevens Journal*, 13 (1989):51.

17. According to Benedetto Croce, "Pure poetry is not sounds which have a logical meaning like the sounds of prose. . .But to say it has no logical meaning is not to say it is a mere physical sound without a soul." Thus, the sense in which I am using the term `self-music' refers to the musical qualities that emerge in the prolonged self-meditations of Stevens' later verse, and the healing effect that such meditations have on his mind. As Emerson wisely observes: "The soul is cured of its maladies by certain incantations" (*The Portable Emerson*, p.258). For the Croce citation, see A. Walton Litz, "Wallace Stevens' Defense of Poetry: `La Poésie Pure', the New Romantic, and the Pressure of Reality," in *Romantic and Modern*, ed. Bornstein, p.119.

18. Eliot's claim that "the man who suffers and the mind which creates" are "completely separate" (*Selected Prose*, p.41), finds its perfect refutation in Stevens' thought and poetry. Stevens' division of the poetic self is, as I argue, purely dialogic, and as such it underscores the constant and dynamic interplay of the conscious and subconscious layers of the mind. According to Miller (*The Linguistic Moment*, p.29), this "dialogue of the mind with itself" constitutes one of the distinguishing characteristics of the modernist literary sensibility, and has its beginnings in the poetry of Arnold and Browing.

19. See, for example, Stevens' poem "The Bouquet," where the optical eye creates `an artifice' or "reality/Of the other eye" (*CP* 448).

20. Du-Hyoung Kang is completely wrong when he says that, "Unlike Mallarmé, Stevens doesn't endevor to reach the transcendent beyond, the realm of ultimate stability and fixity" ("Mallarmé and Wallace Stevens," p.43). To say this is to willfully ignore the essential meaning of the lines just cited, or to misread the general tenor of a poem such as "This Solitude of Cataracts."

21. According to Bloom (*Wallace Stevens*, p.358), in Stevens "The ear goes beyond hearing, into the last things."

22. As Sypher observes, the modernist mind "speaks to the mind without much reference to concrete image or object" (*Rococo to Cubism*, p.317).

23. Quoted in F.O.Mathiessen, *The Achievement of T.S. Eliot* (New York: Oxford University Press), 90.

24. Although Stevens arrives at such a state of mind through a different venue, the end result is similar to what the Symbolists themselves aspire to: "Language is used both symbolically and also musically as a kind of magic aimed at creating a state of trance whence will rise the unheard music, the vision of the absolute." See Joseph Chiari, *Symbolism from Poe to Mallarmé: The Growth of a Myth* (New York: Gordian Press, 1970), p.144.

25. Bevis' main thesis in *Mind of Winter* is that Stevens' radical perceptions and disjunctions, as for example, in "The Snow Man" and most of the longer poems, reflect a lifelong inner struggle to attain a meditative consciousness as propounded by the great Eastern religious mystics. See his "Postscript: Stevens, Meditation, and Modernism," pp.300-314.

26. According to Rilke, "It is not only the *hearable* in music that is important (something can be pleasant to hear without being *true*). What is decisive in all the arts, is not their outward appearance, not what is called the `beautiful'; but rather their deepest, most inner origin, the buried reality that calls forth this appearance" (*Selected Poetry*, p.337).

27. Mallarmé, *Selected Prose Poems, Essays and Letters*, p. 91.

28. For a detailed and highly informative overview of the critical debate pertaining to Stevens' theory and use of metaphor see Brogan, *Stevens and Simile*, pp.3-26. Although the debate has now taken a clearly deconstructionist turn, I have opted to frame my argument solely on the basis of Stevens' views on metaphor, so as to be able to establish the extent to which such views are validated by the canon.

29. Regueiro rejects Stevens' use of metaphor (*The Limits of Imagination*, p.183) on the grounds that it "is ultimately a faking of reality," and that "the object is posed into `this' or `that'—always into something that violates its `thingness'." She obviously chooses to overlook the true aim of Stevens' metaphors, which is to transform things into poetic fictions.

30. According to Louis Mackey, The "human intellect. . .yearns for unity. Our minds want to get behind the duplicity of the proposition to a single simple apprehension of truth. . .What is [in metaphor] an extraordinary unity, a condensation approaching the simplicity of vision." See "On Terms and Terminations: The Dissolution of the Medieval Metaphor," *Texas Quarterly*, 21 (1978): 80-81.

31. Suzanne Jusasz, *Metaphor and the Poetry of Williams, Pound, and Stevens* (Lewisburg: Bucknell University Press, 1974), p.39.

32. For an in-depth discussion of the philosophical aspects of metaphor Nietzsche, Hulme, and Remy de Gourmont as related to twentieth-century modernist poetics, see Schwartz, *The Matrix of Modernism*, pp.73-102.

33. Brogan, *Stevens and Simile*, pp.52-53. As she points out in her perceptive reading of "World without Particularity," it is on account of his powerful use of metaphors that for Stevens eventually,

    The poverty of dirt, the thing upon his breast,
    The hating woman, the meaningless place,
    Become a single being, sure and true.

    (*CP* 454)

34. *Poets of Reality*, pp.240,241.

35. David Walker, *The Transparent Lyric: Reading and Meaning in the Poetry of Wallace Stevens* (Princeton, N.J.: Princeton University Press, 1984), p.68.

36. In an effort to justify Stevens' uses and abuses of metaphorical language, a number of his critics make an attempt to provide a theoretical basis for it; for example, according to Leonard and Wharton, the kind of `reality' that emerges from Stevens' metaphors "is revealed as fictional, but not because it falsifies: the structure of the `real' is bound up with the figural structurings of thought" (*The Fluent Mundo*, p.14). On the other hand, Hillis Miller's valuation of Stevens' uses of metaphor is forceful, critically honest, and to the point: "If the imagination should start out bravely to reach the pineapple by listing all its metaphors, it would never reach its goal. It would become a kind of poetic computer set to explore the permutations of an infinitely variable equation. Day and night, it would still click out its answers. . . To possess the pineapple by going away from it toward the things it

resembles is as hopeless as to try to reach the center of an infinite circle by going around its circumference. . .Metaphor and perspectivism [so used] are instruments of escaping and must be rejected" (*Poets of Reality*, pp.243-44,245).

37. As Walker points out, "without metaphor there is no truth to perceive," so that "Imaginative perception is for Stevens essential to self-definition and self-renewal" (*The Transparent Lyric*, pp.70,73). Also, according to Glauco Cambon, in his poetry Stevens "endevors to root himself in Being through language" (*The Inclusive Flame*, p.119).

38. It is worth noting that what interests Eliot also in metaphorical language is its music: "It is a mistake to suppose that a simile or metaphor is always something meant to be *visible* to the imagination. . . There is the element of rationality, the element of precision, and there is also the element of vagueness which may be used; and we must remember that one distinction between poetry and prose is this, that in poetry the word, each word by itself, though only being fully itself in context, has absolute value. Poetry is *incantation*, as well as imagery" (Eliot's emphasis). Quoted in Bush, *T.S. Eliot*, pp.175-76.

39. Fischer, *The Necessity of Art*, p.91.

40. Schopenhauer quoted in Bloom, *The Sacred Truths*, p.200.

41. Although he rejects surrealism on the grounds that it is only capable of "inventing" and not "discovering" (*OP* 177), in his essay "The Irrational Element in Poetry," Stevens praises the surrealist poets for their irrationality and aliveness: "They concentrate their prowess in a technique which seems singularly limited but which, for all that, exhibits the dynamic influence of the irrational. They are extraordinarily alive and thus they make it possible for us to read poetry that seems filled with gaiety and youth" (*OP* 228).

42. Schwartz, *Matrix of Modernism*, p.85.

43. *Philosophy and Truth: Selections from Nietzche's Notebook of the Early 1870's*, ed. and trans. Daniel Breazeale (Atlantic Highlands. N.J.: Humanities Press, 1979), pp.88-89. It was Remy de Gourmont, the first modern literary critic, who identified the associative or creative power of metaphors in a modernist context: "There are no ideas so remote, no images so incongruous, that an easy freedom of association cannot join them at least for the moment." Quoted in Schwartz, *Matrix of Modernism*, p.84. However, it was Shelley who first stressed the vital importance of metaphorical language in poetry: "[A Poet's] language is vitally metaphorical; that is, it marks the before unapprehended relations of things and perpetuates their apprehension until the words which represent them become, through time, signs for portions or classes of thoughts instead of pictures of integral thoughts . . .Language itself is poetry; and to be a poet is to apprehend the true and the beautiful." See *Shelley's Prose*, ed. David Lee Clark (Albuquerque: University of New Mexico Prees, 1954), pp.278-79.

44. Ernst Cassirer, *An Essay on Man: An Introduction to a Philosophy of Human Culture* (Garden City, N.Y.: Anchor Books, 1953), p.186.

45. According to twentieth-century existential philosophers, there is no inherent stability or coherence in rational thought either; thus, for Karl Jaspers, "Reason has no assured stability: it is constantly on the move. Once it has gained a position it presses on to criticize it . . .It presses on constantly to the place where unity is broken through in order that in this break-through it may grasp the truth that is in it." See *A Dictionary of Existentialism*, compliled and arranged by Ralph B. Winn, (New York: The Philosophical Library, 1960), p.90.

46. Jacques Maritain, *Creative Intuition in Art and Poetry* (New York: Meridian Books, 1955), p.57.

47. Charles Baudelaire, *Selected Verse*, Trans. Francis Scarfe (Harmondsworth, Middlesex: Penguin, 1961), p.192.

48. *A Vision* (London: Macmillan, 1962), p.268.

49. Maritain, *Creative Intuition*, pp.53,55.

50. *From Baudelaire to Surrealism*, p.318.

51. Ibid., 318-319.

52. See Ashley Brown and Robert S. Haller, eds., *The Achievement of Wallace Stevens* (New York: Lippincott, 1962), p.207.

53. Ibid., 202. Stevens' partiality for the irrational in poetry very often takes on the tone of a manifesto: "Poetry must be irrational" (*OP* 162); "For the poet, the irrational is elemental" (*OP* 229); "There is a point at which intelligence destroys poetry" (*L* 305); "Pure poetry is both mystical and irrational" (*OP* 222); "The poem must resist the intelligence/Almost successfully" (*CP* 350).

54. For a different interpretation of the `giant' in Stevens, see Joseph G. Kronick, "Large White Man Reading: Stevens' Genealogy of the Giant," *The Wallace Stevens Journal* 7 (1983): 89-98.

55. Bloom believes that the poem, among other things, is also an attack against Eliot's poetic idiom (*Wallace Stevens*, p.226). If this is so, what Stevens probably had in mind were Eliot's views on language expressed in "Burnt Norton" (*Four Quartets*, p.19):

     Words strain,
     Crack and sometimes break, under the burden,
     Under the tension, slip, slide, perish,

     Decay with imprecision, will not stay in place,
     Will not stay still.

56. It is worth noting that Stevens uses the very same imagery in describing the essence of a nonhuman divinity in "Less and Less Human, O Savage Spirit":

> *If there must be a god in the house, must be,*
> *Saying things in the rooms and on the stair,*
>
> *Let him move as the sunlight moves on the floor,*
> *Or moonlight, silently, as Plato's ghost*
>
> *Or Aristotle's skeleton. Let him hang out*
> *His stars on the wall. He must dwell quietly.*

   (CP 327)

57. Quoted in Brown and Haller, *The Achievement of Wallace Stevens*, p.206.

58. J. Hillis Miller, "Wallace Stevens' Poetry of Being," in Pearce and Miller, *The Act of the Mind*, p.141.

59. Leggett, *Wallace Stevens and Poetic Theory*, pp.41,119.

60. Valery, *The Art of Poetry*, p.64.

CHAPTER IV

"An Ordinary Evening in New Haven":
The Ultimate Mind Poem

> It is not an empty clearness, a bottomless sight.
> It is a visibility of thought,
> In which hundreds of eyes, in one mind, see at once.
> > Wallace Stevens, "An Ordinary Evening in New Haven"

Unlike "Notes Toward a Supreme Fiction," its major rival in the canon, "An Ordinary Evening in New Haven" has over the years received mixed critical appraisals from Stevens' comentators, ranging from overly high praise (Bloom) to total rejection (Vendler).[1] The reason for such a wide spectrum of critical opinion is due as much to the poem's inherent difficulties as to the critics' own attitude in facing up to the challenge of these difficulties. Their confusion arises mainly from their insistence to read the poem in rational terms, or with a strong theoretical bias, thus ignoring Stevens' warning precept—clearly voiced in "The Creations of Sound"—that poetry comes `of its own, without understanding, in sounds not chosen'. The main reason for a lack of consensus as to the general standing of the poem in the canon—as is the case with "Notes toward a Supreme Fiction"—is because the critics' valuations of the poem to date have been either embarrassingly evasive or downright tautological. Thus, according to one critic, the poem is "an act of continual self-creation," whose unity "is the unity of its diverse style";[2] and for another, it constitutes "a translation of its elemental feeling," in the sense that it "is imitative of nothing actual or possible."[3] And finally, in the words of a third

169

commentator, the poem "scatters and weaves a vision of poetry as being that which sticks or adheres as poetry."[4] It seems, then, that as a poetic text "An Ordinary Evening in New Haven" resists mostly those critics who bring to bear on their interpretations of it a set critical approach or theory, which eventually makes their `rational' reading of the poem schematic, unconvincing and, in the worst of cases, incongruous.

In order to avail ourselves then, most profitably of its meanings so as to be able to assess it as a poetic text, I believe that the only way to read "An Ordinary Evening in New Haven" is to do so on the basis of two closely related premises: firstly, to look at it as the crowning achievement of Stevens' long career as a poetic perspectivist, which began auspiciously with "The Comedian as the Letter C" in 1922; and secondly, to accept it as the very apotheosis of Stevens' conception of poetry as an act of the mind. The first thing that must be said about the poem is that its involuted perspectivism stems directly from Stevens' own structureless, fluid, and volatile perceptions of reality; which means that Stevens' sense of self and world is so fluctuant and unstable that all his ideas, thoughts, perceptions or flashing intuitions are invariably reduced to "a point of relation within an infinite complex of relations;" so that what might be said to constitute his stable view of life, in the end it turns out to be "a self-contradictory privileging of either external reality or the individual mind."[5] And it is this unceasing perspectivizing of Stevens' poetic mind[6] which accounts for the complex dialectic of "An Ordinary Evening in New Haven"; a dialectic which, according to Delmore Schwartz's penetrating insight, constitutes "a system of perspectives" which "can make anything and everything poetic" at any given moment.[7] It is, however, such a complex way of writing verse that its undecipherable intricacies of style and language point to the kind of poetic landscape where poetry goes "beyond poetry," in fact to such an extreme degree, that in the end "Poetic form is made to negate itself";[8] which is to say, its meanings are no longer paraphrasable or accessible for instructive critical discourse. Conceived and written on such a scale of complexity, what "This endlessly elaborating poem" (*CP* 486) finally reveals to the reader is a mind given to the momentous task of expanding "the field of consciousness further and further," so that "it lose[s] itself in the ineffable."[9]

Given then, its strong perspectivist stance, one can look at "An Ordinary Evening in New Haven" and see it for what it really is: Stevens' most ambitious treatise on poetry of the mind in verse; in short, a poem in which, once again, Stevens must proceed to `throw away the lights' in order to let his spirit's alchemicana work its verbal magic of trope, image, and sound `in the dark.'[10] And the poem's thirty-one cantos—or 558 lines of verse—of highly internalized and mostly disconnected meditations,[11] provide Stevens' profuse imagination with ample room in which to work to its fullest capacity such magic. As for the urge that engenders and sustains these meditations, it answers Stevens' obsessive need to find what is `real' and `unreal'; which makes his mind ceaselessly oscillate between the phenomenal and the noumenal, the immanent and the transcendent, brute fact and intuitive essence.[12] In the final analysis, it is in these endlessly ongoing shifts in perception—"in the movement of the colors of the mind" and "transcripts of feeling" (*CP* 466,479)—that the poem's mersmerizing, and at times haunting music has its source. As for the validity of Stevens' epistemological cogitations that are carried on in the course of the poem, they simply provide his `never-resting mind' with the kind of free play whereby it might hopefully find `what will suffice.'[13]

Part of a larger European poetic tradition, Stevens' poetry of the mind, as examplified in his intricately discursive meditations in "An Ordinary Evening in New Haven," is grounded almost entirely in a new "logic of consciousness;"[14] that is, in a radical way of apprehending reality which originated with the Romantics' mystical urge to explore `unknown modes of being' (Wordsworth), was later refined upon by the Symbolists, and finally given free play by the French Surrealist poets in the 20s and 30s. Drawing its strength mainly from the use of intuitive or "omnimodal"[15] perceptions and its aesthetic "exultation of the irrational,"[16] the impelling force behind this new poetic `logic' was an intense need to discover fresh modalities of thought and feeling hitherto unknown to the rational mind; in fact this urge was so strong that the language in which these modalities were expressed became fraught with transcendental meanings. As a result, and following the `revolution of the word' brought about by the Symbolist and Surrealist poets, poetic language now became a privileged medium to the point where it came to be viewed by a large number of philosophical humanists and literary scholars as an agent of "ontological revelation";[17] which is to say, language was now not only looked upon as "a source of meaning [but] also as a source of being."[18] In the end, carried away by their own grandiloquent claims and visionary trust in the power or words, these humanists and scholars came to regard poetic language as "the house of Being,"[19] and, in some cases, "as a quasireligious object" in itself.[20]

In "An Ordinary Evening in New Haven" Stevens uses this radical poetic logic to its fullest creative potential in order to intensify and sustain the interiority of his meditations; but he does so not for the mere purpose of creating for himself the illusion of a transcendent inwardness—as is the case with Rilke, who often "mistakes his own tropes as spiritual evidences"[21]—but as a means of actually augmenting and experiencing such inwardness as the very ground of an ontologically renewed immanence.[22] And for Stevens, the possibility of such a renewal lies entirely in the power of words, that is, in the fortuitous inception of new tropes and `irrational' flashes of intuitive perception.[23] Looking then, at "An Ordinary Evening in New Haven" as Stevens' most exemplary poem of the mind, that is, as a poetic act that sustains itself almost exclusively on the irrational-intuitive plane of his sensibility, we are able to understand better the "density"[24] of its style and language; which is to say, we are now critically prepared to accommodate its discontinuous thought processec, blurred allusions, and intricate syntax[25] which, thankfully, is occasionally made comprehensible by its brilliantly concise and telling apercus.[26] Thus, we can say that in the final analysis "the true hero" in the poem "is [its] language";[27] a `hero' in the sense that language is no longer the means but the end of poetic discourse; that is, it is now identified with the mind's deepest ontological urges, and therefore it becomes its most vital source of self-renewal. As Stevens says in one of his most characteristic verses, "The poem refreshes life" (*CP* 382), except that the `freshness' in question does not signify an Adamic urge, but rather refers to the revitalizing effect or inner transformation that poetic perception brings to bear on the creative self:

> *The freshness of transformation is*
> *The freshness of a world. It is our own,*
> *It is ourselves, the freshness of ourselves.* (*CP* 397-98)

What Stevens says here quite clearly is that the self's true transformation resides only in imaginative experience,[28] that is, in the poetic act itself and the profound effect it has on the poet's mind:

> *The way a poet feels when he is writing, or after he has*
> *written, a poem that completely accomplishes his purposes*
> *is evidence of the personal nature of his activity. To*

173

describe it by exaggerating it, he shares the transformation, not to say apotheosis, accomplished by the poem. It must be this experience that makes him think of poetry as possibly a phase of metaphysics (NA 49).[29]

However, this poetry of mind as self-transformation or `cure' that Stevens advocates here so fervently has no definite subject that we can speak of, a fact fully attested by our reading of "An Ordinary Evening in New Haven." So we can safely say that, in the final analysis, what constitutes the "real subject" of such verse is "the act of writing" itself;[30] or, more specifically, "the poetic act" as pure afflatus, "the flare-up of being in the imagination."[31] In other words, what truly obtains in a mind poem as conceived by Stevens is the creative heat, the miraculous birth of pristine perception married to image and word which, through "an infinite series of transformations," enables the poet to revitalize his perceptual powers and thus become "sufficient unto himself."[32] And what needs to be stressed about "An Ordinary Evening in New Haven" in this respect is this: that what it really dramatizes, projects, and gloriously celebrates is the mind's attempt at perceptual and ontological regeneration;[33] an attempt exemplified by Professor Eucalyptus' urge to try and find `god in the object itself'; and it is this urge that establishes his common poetic lineage with Stevens' other kindred personas such as Crispin, `the man with the blue guitar', the androgynous Mrs Alfred Uruguay, Hans Richter, and Canon Aspirin. Eucalyptus then is Stevens' veteran perspectivist with rich experience in inner fragmentation and intense visionary aspirations for order and wholeness; a man who, continuing to live "In a world forever without a plan" (*OP* 76), still aspires towards a vision of `vivid transparence', dedicated stubbornly to the momentous task of ordering his "Confused illuminations" and "disembodied images" (*CP* 466,460) into mind poems, convinced that such fragments, so fused, can have "their glittering crown" (*CP* 460).[34] In short, his is a mind which, caught in its own psychic fixities, can only escape from them by "Turn[ing] to its own figurations" and "speaking the poem as it is," impelled by the belief that it can thus "renew(s) the world [and itself] in a verse" (*CP* 246, 473, *OP* 103).

But there is a more positive side to Professor Eucalyptus' erratic phenomenology and disarrayed mind, revealed to us in "Large Red Man Reading" (*CP* 423), Stevens' last major persona. In this poem Stevens paints for us his last self-portrait, where he poses as an Ariel-like figure, `swaddled in revery', who "speaks like a man reasoning with himself in solitude"[35] fully convinced that "the portents of his own powers [are] the only portents he would ever know."[36] In other words, Stevens presents himself here as the quintessential perspectivist poet whose mind, totally entranced by the music of its own meditations,[37] is able to conjure up in words that `vivid transparence' his spirit so strongly craves for. And this transparence is projected for us in what was to be Stevens' last poem:

> *The palm at the end of the mind,*
> *Beyond the last thought, rises*
> *In the bronze decor,*
> *A gold-feathered bird*
> *Sings in the palm, without human meaning,*
> *Without human feeling, a foreign song.*
> *You know then that it is not the reason*
> *That makes us happy or unhappy.*
> *The bird sings. Its feathers shine.*
> *The palm stands on the edge of space.*
> *The wind moves slowly in the branches.*
> *The bird's fire-fangled feathers dangle down.* (PM 398)

"Of Mere Being" is Stevens' death-bed vision of what reality is for him—'a palm on the edge of space,' or `a gold-feathered bird' whose song is totally `without human meaning'. What he does, of course, by visualizing reality in such terms is to create for himself an imaginative construct that allows his to resolve all his dualities and contraries, thus providing him with a saving refuge from that terrifying `visibility of thought'—the perspectivist's curse—'in which hundreds of eyes, in one mind, see at once.' As for the poem's ultimate meaning, I believe that its true clue lies in the phrase `bronze decor', which I take to be a trope for stasis, order, and permanence or final being—in other words, death; an inner urge whose thematic antecedent is to be found in Stevens' strong desire, expressed in "This Solitude of Cataracts": "To be a bronze man/. . .Breathing his bronzen breath at the azury centre of time" (*CP* 425).[38]

In concluding then this treatise, and taking our cue from the stripped purity, in-depth vision, and staying power of Stevens' last lyric, we can say of him that, as a poet who `helps us live our lives,' and on account of his lifelong devotion to poetry, proves Arnold correct, who had warned us that as post-Christians we would "have to turn to poetry to interpret life for us, to console us, to sustain us."[39] As Stevens himself puts it more eloquently: "the wonder and mystery of art, as indeed of religion in the last resort, is the revelation of something `wholly other' by which the inexpressible loneliness of thinking is broken and enriched" (*OP* 237).[40] And it is this passionate belief in the power of poetry to satisfy "The desire for celestial ease in the heart" (*CP* 467), that in the end turns poetry, for Stevens, into a kind of holiness wherein

> *There* [is] *no fury in transcendent forms.*
> *But his actual candle blaze*[s] *with artifice.*
> (*CP* 523)

A Cure of the Mind

NOTES

1. According to Bloom (*Wallace Stevens*, p.253), the poem is "a majestic performance," whereas in Vendler's estimation it is "almost unremittingly minimal, and over and over again threatens to die of its own starvation. . .It is, humanly speaking, the saddest of all Stevens' poems" (*On Extended Wings*, pp.269-70). On the other hand, Riddel chooses to stand on middle ground: according to him, "It is a brilliant display of metaphors and similes," but "is not successful as a total poem" (*The Clairvoyant Eye*, p.263). For other major critical readings of the poem see Carroll, *A New Romanticism*, pp. 275-99; Walker, *The Transparent Lyric*, pp.107-16; and Merle E. Brown, *Wallace Stevens: The Poem as Act* (Detroit: Wayne State University Press, 1970), pp.195-204.

2. Riddel, *The Clairvoyant Eye*, pp.258, 263.

3. Brown, *Wallace Stevens: The Poem as Act*, p.202.

4. Bloom, *Wallace Stevens*, pp.331-32.

5. Carroll, *A New Romanticism*, pp.286,282. In this respect, the perspectivist affinities between Stevens' poetry and Emerson's prose become evident; as David Wyatt perceptively observes, "In following the verbal action of `Circles' we can discover ourselves becoming active souls. We are processed by a structure aspiring at once to closure and continuity. While reading `Circles' we enjoy a sense of resolved being and unstayed becoming." See Jane P. Tompkins, ed., *Reader-Response Criticism: From Formalism to Post-Structuralism* (Baltimore and London: The Johns Hopkins University Press, 1992), p.272.

6. In his perceptive study of the poet, *Wallace Stevens: A World of Transforming Shapes* (Lewisburg:Bucknell University Press, 1976), p.24, Alan Perlis asks the seemingly innocuous, but in fact momentous, question: "Why does Stevens engage in such play?"

A Cure of the Mind

This is one of the crucial questions that I have been trying to answer in this essay. I believe that it is the kind of play of mind and sensibility that allows Stevens to reaffirm his poetic powers and thereby renew himself ontologically.

7. "In the Orchards of the Imagination," in *Stevens: The Critical Heritage*, ed. Doyle, p.402.

8. Pearce, *The Continuity of American Poetry*, pp.413,381.

9. The statement is by Henry James quoted in Kazin, *An American Procession*, p.174. The full meaning and relevance of Stevens' cognate statement quoted at the beginning of my essay—'the extension of the mind beyond the range of the mind'—now becomes clear. It is worth noting that St. John Perse's poetic aim was also to achieve "a very allusive and mysterious play. . .at the extreme verge of what consciousness can grasp." See Arthur J. Knodel, *Saint John Perse: A Study of His Poetry* (Edinburgh: Edinburgh University Press, 1966), p.58.

10. See "The Man with the Blue Guitar," canto xxxii (*CP* 183), where Stevens urges us to use the irrational as an effective means of jettisoning our inherited and inert perceptions of self and world. Specifically, the use of the irrational in poetry allows the "*inversion of logical categories, proliferation of ambivalences*, irradiation with a resulting *annexation of other images*, and above all the power to offer *richer suggestions at each reading*" (emphasis mine). See Gaston Bachelard, *On Poetic Imagination and Reverie*, trans. Colette Gaudin (New York: Bobbs-Merrill, 1971), p.xxxv.

11. Helen Vendler complains that Stevens' quasi-philosophical meditations create "a poetry of disconnection," and goes on to say that "If this is a poetry of meditation, it does not have the sustained progressive development that we know in other meditative poets" (*On Extended Wings*, pp.65,71). It seems to me,

178

on the basis of this valuation, that Vendler has not quite grasped the intricate workings of Stevens' poetry of the mind.

12. Stevens' "perpetual meditation" (*CP* 466) or sudden shifts in perception, allow him to experience a feeling of self-transcendence. As Geoffrey Hartman points out in describing the same process in Wordsworth, it "is the confluence, the almost imperceptible confluence, of mind and external reality which. . .reveals the transcendent principle blending both." See *The Unmediated Vision: An Interpretation of Wordsworth, Hopkins, Rilke, and Valery* (New York: Harcourt, Brace, 1966), p.25.

13. As Robert Rehder puts it, in commenting upon Stevens' strong tendency to reduce all ideas to poetic play: "Although he [Stevens] plays with the concepts of ontology and epistemology as he plays with the idea of religion and the idea of system, the play is more important to him than the system"; moreover, this allows Stevens "the most freedom, the most opportunities for improvisation and for changing his point of view." See *The Poetry of Wallace Stevens* (New York: St. Martin's Press, 1988), p.220.

14. Susanne Langer quoted in Hamburger, *The Truth of Poetry*, p.26. Cf. Eliot's phrase `a logic of the imagination' already cited.

15. George Santayana, *Scepticism and Animal Faith* (New York: Dover Publications, 1955), p.69.

16. Erich Kahler, *The Disintegration of Form in the Arts* (New York: George Brazilier, 1968), p.30. As Rehder (*Wallace Stevens*, p.220) points out, in Stevens' case the "so-called irrational" allows him to give vent to "unconscious articulations" and thus make possible "the coexistence [and reconciliation] of contradictions." In other words, it makes for a "deepened speech" or "greater aptitude and apprehension" (CP 387).

17. Lentricchia, *After the New Criticism*, p.97.

18. Bachelard, *On Poetic Imagination and Reverie*, p.xx.

19. Heidegger quoted in Walter Kaufmann, *From Shakespeare to Existentialism* (Garden City, N.Y.: Anchor Books, 1960), p.339. For Heidegger's views on poetry and language, see *Poetry, Language, Thought*, trans. Albert Hofstadter (New York: Harper & Row, 1971), pp. 213-29.

20. Hartman, *Criticism in the Wilderness*; p. 117. A large number of literary critics in the 60s, before their defection to deconstructionism, shared Heidegger's quasi-mystical views on poetry and language. Thus, according to Hillis Miller (*Poets of Reality*, p.283), "man participates in being through words," while Glauco Cambon (*The Inclusive Flame*, p.119) looks upon the modern poet as a man who "endevors to root himself in Being through language."

21. Bloom, *The Sacred Truths*, p.200.

22. Stevens refers to this condition of renewed immanence or perceptual freshness as "vivid transparence" (*CP* 380); and this is what the phrase connotes for Frank Lentricchia: "This supreme, because unmediated, consciousness would effect original relation to things, face-to-face, abstracted from all tradition. Vivid transparence would yield access to what Stevens called, in urgent redundancy, `living changingness,' the medium of escape from granite monotony, the culturally enforced repetitions of what has been thought and said. The pleasure achieved would be `peace,' a moment attendant upon a `crystallization of freshness': vivid, living changingness aesthetically trapped, as in a crystal, known in and for its uniqueness, then quickly lost in its freshness, having been hardened in verbal form. Vivid transparence is both medium and substance of authentic literariness: avant-garde of perception and perpetual ground of the new, perpetually imperiled by the forms of cultural habit, an imperative constantly to reimagine."

See *Modernist Quartet* (Cambridge, N.Y.: Cambridge University Press, 1994), p.75.

23. According to Maritain, it is "The poetic sense [of things] that gleams in the dark. This poetic sense, which is but one with poetry itself, is the inner, ontological entelechy of the poem, and gives it its very being and substantial significance" (*Creative Intuition*, p.54). It is worth noting that Maritain also uses the phrase `in the dark', as Stevens does, in order to stress the irrational element in poetry.

24. "Density is very often something that strikes the ear rather than the eye; it is often something you hear happening to voices as they modify words and phrases which, at another point, seemed quite clear or casual. Density is usually accompanied not by the extruding allusiveness of modernism but by the covert allusiveness of troping. Troping gives evidence of the human involvement in the shaping of language, and it prevents language from imposing itself upon us with the force and indifference of a Technology. It frees us from predetermined meanings. Troping is the turning of a word in directions or detours it seemed destined otherwise to avoid" (Poirier, *The Renewal of Literature*, p.231).

25. According to Jascha Kessler ("Wallace Stevens: Entropical Poet," p.85), "all of Stevens' notorious mights, woulds, maybes, perhapses, and as ifs are concealing a fundamental No, concealing that No in plain sight, like the purloined letter."

26. As Beverly Coyle points out in her study of Stevens' aphoristic style, *A Thought to be Rehearshed: Aphorism in Wallace Stevens's Poetry* (Ann Arbor, Mich.: UMI Research Press, 1983), p.25, for Stevens, "aphorisms have an affinity with the fragmentlike nature of experience," and thus express his "tendency to experience life as a complex series of interacting congeries." Lentricchia also gives us an intimate glimpse of Stevens' use of language in his longer poems as related to the perspectivist aspect of his poetic mind:

A Cure of the Mind

"What he is writing is a kind of pre-poetry, a tentative approach to the poem, an enactment of desire, not as a state of mind, with all the inert implications of the phrase "state of mind," but as movement, and not movement in a straight line, as if he could see the end of the journey, but a zigzag sort of motion: desire as improvisational action, a jazz poetry that gives us a sense of starting, stopping, changing direction, revising the phrase, refining the language, drafting the poem and keeping the process of drafting all *there* as the final thing because the finished thing can not be bad" (*Modernist Quartet*, p.160).

27. Litz, *Introspective Voyager*, p.125.

28. Although, as Coleridge claims, "all objects are essentially fixed and dead," ultimately, in terms of poetic creation, `freshness' does not reside in things as they are but in our perception of them, so that the visual vividness of `a red wheelbarrow glazed with rain' eventually becomes an imaginative experience with strong ontological undertones; an experience which, according to Pound, gives us a "sense of sudden liberation from the limits and space limits. . . [a] sense of sudden growth." Quoted in Schneidau, *Ezra Pound*, p.21. For the Coleridge citation see *Biographia Literaria*, ed George Watson (New York: Dutton, 1956), p.167.

29. Cf. Norman Mailer's own view concerning the creative process in "Norman Mailer: An Interview," *The Paris Review*, 31 (1964):58: "The only time I know that something is true is at the moment I discover it in the act of writing. I think it's that. I think it's the moment of intellection, this moment of seizure when one knows it's true. One may not have written it well enough for others to know, but you're in love with the truth when you discover it at the point of a pencil. That in and by itself is one of the few rare pleasures in life."

30. Richard Ellmann and Charles Feidelson, J., eds., *The Modern Tradition: Backgrounds of Modern Literature* (New York: Oxford

University Press, 1965), p.13. Bradbury and Ruland (*From Puritanism to Postmodernism*, p.247) express the same idea in a roundabout way: "Stevens' poems were always based in an act of thought, always subject to the occasions that prompted them, always tuned as instruments of aesthetic delight."

31. Bachelard, *Poetic Imagination and Reverie*. p.73.

32. Pearce, *Continuity of American Poetry*, p.377. As Rehder points out, in underscoring the ontological aspect of Stevens' poetry of the mind: "The poem of the act of the mind is the poem of the mind committed to a self-sustaining process of composing itself, to action in support of being (*The Poetry of Wallace Stevens*, p.220)." Finally, it is this ontological or solipsistic aspect of Stevens's poetic imagination that distinguishes it from that of Coleridge; thus according to Riddel, "Stevens' imagination, one might add here, is not a `shaping spirit' in the Coleridgean sense, but only in the sense of its transformative power over the phenomena of mind" (*The Clairvoyant Eye*, p.282). As Stevens himself puts it: "There is nothing that exists exclusively by reason of the imagination. [The imagination] does not create except as it transforms" (*L* 364).

33. There is a long tradition of earth-worshippers in Western literature whose main representatives are Hölderlin and Wordsworth ("Earth, I love you!"), Rilke ("Earth, my dearest"), Hopkins ("Earth, sweet Earth"), Gide (*The Fruits of the Earth*), and Lawrence (*The Rainbow*), but Stevens is not one of them. Swayed by the lush paganism of "Sunday Morning" and a few short lyrics of a similar vein, some of Stevens' early critics wished to have us believe that his verse projects a "summer vision of life" (Frye) and celebrates "the poetry of earth" (Bloom, *Wallace Stevens*, p.195), and that therefore his sole "allegiance is to earth" (Doggett, *Stevens' Poetry of Thought*, p.ix). In making such sweeping valuations, they have obviously overlooked the bleak vision and meaning expressed in these lines from "World without Peculiarity":

A Cure of the Mind

What good is it that the earth is justified,
That it is complete, that it is an end,
That in itself it is enough?   (CP 453)

For sources of citations, see Hölderlin and Mörike: *Selected Poems*, p.9; Rilke, *Selected Poetry*, p.203; Hopkins, *Poems*, p.240; and Northrop Frye, "The Realistic Oriole: A Study of Wallace Stevens, in *Stevens: A Collection of Critical Essays*, ed. Borroff, p.165. For a reading of Heidegger as a philosophical earth-woshipper, see F. Joseph Smith, "In-the-World and On-the-Earth: A Heideggerian Interpretation," in *Heidegger and the Quest for Truth*, ed. Frings, pp.184-203.

34. In a general evaluation of "An Ordinary Evening in New Haven" as a modernist poetic text, one could say that it evinces a capacity—to use Valery's phrase—for "maximum possibility and maximum capacity for incoherence" (*Monsieur Teste*, p.73). As for the poem's complex tropes and language, "One can intuit the radius of [their] connotations, but one is hard put to define that radius (Hölderlin and Mörike: *Selected Poems*, p.xxii.)

35. Eliot uses the words to describe the mind of the English poet Sir John Davies (1569-1626). See *On Poetry and Poets* (New York: Farrar, Strauss and Cudahy, 1957), p.242.

36. James Benziger, *Images of Eternity: Studies in the Poetry of Religious Vision from Wordsworth to T.S. Eliot* (Carbondale, Ill.; Southern Illinois University Press, 1964), p.242.

37. Cf. Eliot's uses of poetry: "the incantatory element is very important. . .It is the words that count, not the feelings about them. When I read poetry myself I put myself in a kind of trance." Quoted in Bush, *T.S. Eliot*, p.123

38. Steven Shaviro offers a considered and perceptive interpretation of the poem's anti-humanist stance and its implications: "The bird in the palm is not ours, it does not call us, but it remains, it

affects us, in its ungraspable and irreducible insistence. Its `mere being' is all that can be affirmed of it. But such an affirmation also marks a death: the death of identity, the death of truth, the death of religious and humanistic values. Are we to see, in this death, in these lines, in such a song, the horror of the void, the nothingness that threatens to submerge the human, or are we to confront, rather, the possibility of a new and inhuman affirmation, the promise of transformation without end, the positivity of this void and this destruction? This new affirmation, which transgresses the limits of our humanism, is obviously not to be attained by mere force or will. But this affirmation already exists, a threat and promise of metamorphosis, an alterity insinuating itself within, the very space of our selfhood and privacy, the positivity of `mere being,' the song of the bird `on the edge of space,' the incessant movement of the `river of rivers' in which, `the mere flowing of the water is a gaiety.'" See "That Which Is Always Beginning: Stevens' Poetry Affirmation," in *Critical Essays on Wallace Stevens*, ed. Axelrod and Deese, p.210.

39.   Matthew Arnold, *Poetry and Criticism*, ed. A. Dwight Culler (Boston: Houghton Mifflin, 1961), p.306.

40.   As Lloyd Frankerberg points out in his general evaluation of Stevens in *Pleasure Dome: On Reading Modern Poetry* (Boston: Houghton Mifflin, 1949), p.267: "Stevens' poetry fulfills and exceeds Matthew Arnold's critical prophecy. It does not supplant the religious impulse. It *is* that impulse, faithfully directed." Murray Krieger touches upon this relation of modern poetry to religion in terms of an either/or proposition: "If we share Arnold's loss of faith, we can go either of two ways: we can view poetry as a human triumph made out of our darkness, as the creation of verbal meaning in the blank universe to serve as a visionary substitute for a defunct religion; or we can—in our negation—extend our faithlessness, the blankness of our universe, to our poetry." Quoted in Lentricchia, *After the New Criticism*, p.212.

APPENDIX

"Not Ideas about the Thing but the Thing Itself"

At the earliest ending of winter,
In March, a scrawny cry from outside
Seemed like a sound in his mind.

He knew that he heard it,
A bird's cry, at daylight or before,
In the early March wind.

The sun was rising at six,
No longer a battered panache above snow...
It would have been outside.

It was not from the vast ventriloquism
Of sleep's faded papier-mâché...
The sun was coming from outside.

That scrawny cry—It was
A chorister whose c preceded the choir.
It was part of the colossal sun,

Surrounded by its choral rings,
Still far away: It was like
A new knowledge of reality. (CP 534)

In conducting his series of interviews (*Criticism in Society*) with some of the foremost contemporary literary theorists and critics,[1] part of Imre Salusinszky's strategy was to request each one of the participants to provide an on-the-spot interpretation of Stevens' poem "Not Ideas about the Thing but the Thing Itself," presumably on the assumption that it constitutes a hallmark of the poet's complexity and therefore worthy of the best possible critical reading. One of the things, however, that one finds objectionable in these interviews is the extent to which each interviewee chooses to interpret the poem in a way that best suits his or her a priori theorizations about literature in general; or, lacking a theory in which to frame their argument, they proceed to bluff their way to what sounds like a plausible interpretation—something that almost all of Stevens' poems allow us to do with impunity. The issue I am raising here is that, considering the range of sophisticated critical response to the poem, none of its commentators here makes an in-depth reference to the canon for possible clues, allusions, or thematic antecedents that might lend validity to their arguments, or help the reader come to a better understanding of Stevens' poetic modalities and, hopefully, of the poem's ultimate meaning. Thus, what we are given instead are critical fabulations, such as Harold Bloom's contention that the poem is a "typical Stevensian modification of the Wordsworthian-Whitmanesque crisis-poem" (p.59); Barbara Johnson's total evasiveness or critical second-guessing; or involuted readings of the poem (Hillis Miller) that tend to further obfuscate rather than help dispel its baffling obscurity. In support of my objections, then, I would like to offer the following canonical guidelines for a more valid interpretation of the poem:

(a) A variant of Stevens' poetry of the mind (as defined in this essay), "Not Ideas about the Thing but the Thing Itself" is written on the premise that "Life is a composite of the propositions about it" (*OP* 171); so that the proper theoretical framework for the poem should be found in a group of poems composed on the same premise, namely:

"Connoisseur of Chaos" (*CP* 215), "So-and-So Reclining on Her Couch" (*CP* 295), "Man Carrying Thing" (*CP* 350), and "On the Road Home" (*CP* 203).

(b) So defined, it follows that the poem's meaning is totally dependent on the rhetorical use of poetic tropes; which is to say, the `new knowledge of reality' Stevens alludes to at the end is only an imaginative construct, the result of verbal play, or what he calls elsewhere "the artifice of a new reality" (*PM* 361). And this notion of reality as "imagined artifice" (*PM* 295) is fully confirmed by Stevens' performance in "Someone Puts a Pineapple Together"—his strongest and most inaccessible mind poem—in which he declares that "Here the total artifice reveals itself/As the total reality" (*PM* 299); or as he puts it in one of his essays: "*the revelation of reality* is inherent in the words" (*OP* 213; Stevens' emphasis). It should be clear, then, that the poem is neither the record of a mystical experience (Benziger, *Images of Eternity*, p.242), nor the expression of an inner crisis, be it Wordsworthian or Whitmansque, as Bloom claims. Thus, what the poem eventually achieves, through Stevens' skillful use of tropes or verbal legerdemain, is the illusion of a new reality.

(c) The pivotal words in the poem directly involved in creating its aura of mystification and opacity, are `colossal sun,' `scrawny cry,' `chorister,' `choir' and `choral rings'. As for Stevens' mannered locutions—'battered panache,' `vast ventriloquism,' `faded papier-mâché—they have no bearing on the poem's ultimate meaning, and only act inadvertently as verbal decoys that distract the reader in his effort to find the poem's true focus.

(d)   Stevens' most endeared and primary symbol, `the colossal sun,' is used here both as a figure of primal life-force and poetry's transforming power—

> *To-morrow when the sun,*
> *For all your images,*
> *Comes up as the sun, bull fire,*
> *Your images will have left*
> *No shadows of themselves—* (OP 198)

a power that Stevens identifies with his own poetic imagination, which "Come(s) from the strength that is the strength of the sun"; so that, eventually,

> *His self and the sun were one*
> *And his poems, although makings of his self,*
> *Were no less makings of the sun.*
> (CP 532)

As for `scrawny cry,' it constitutes the poem's rhetorical pivot which makes it a typical proposition-poem. Is the cry `real' or `unreal,' actual or imaginary? In other words, does it come from the throat of an actual bird or the depths of Stevens' somnolent mind? And it is the answer we choose to give to this question that our `new knowledge of reality' presumably depends on. But the question itself proves to be rhetorical in that—and here is the crux of my argument—whether posited as real or the result of a hallucinatory experience, `cry' stands as a synecdoche for Stevens' act-of-the-mind imagination; since it impels him to write his poem of the mind and thereof experience a new `knowledge of reality'. Also, by troping cry into a `chorister,' Stevens wants to make us aware of the inner

189

music that will eventually emerge through the process of composing a mind poem about the hallucinatory experience of having heard a scrawny cry. As for the chorister's `c' that precedes `choir,' it is only Stevens' patented way of playing with words, as is the case in "The Comedian with the Letter C."

(e) With reference to the word `choir' and its plural, `choral rings,' they refer to the process of poetic transformation (the `spirit's alchemicana') as enacted in Stevens poetry of the mind, and particularly his radical use of tropes from which his distinctive verbal music emerges. This interpretation finds its perfect gloss in "Credences of Summer":

> *And the secondary senses of the ear*
> *Swarm, not with secongary sounds, but choirs,*
> *Not evocations but last choirs, last sounds*
> *With nothing else compounded, carried full,*
> *Pure rhetoric of a language without words.*
> (CP 374)

Needless to say, as an oxymoron, `pure rhetoric of a language without words' describes perfectly the kind of language Stevens invents in his mind poems.

(f) Finally, for the actual referent of the word `thing' mentioned in the title, it must be identified with the poetic process as an `act of the mind whereby, through the sheer play of tropes, an auditory experience is turned into a `new' apprehension of reality, thus fulfilling Stevens' desire to discover, in his own patented empirico-mystical manner, "God in the object itself" (CP 475).[2] And this, I suppose, answers the challenging question that Salusinszky posed to one of his interviewees: "What is this poet [Stevens] trying to do for himself. . .by writing this poem?" (p.60).

Notes

1. Harold Bloom, Jacques Derrida, Northrop Frye, Barbara Johnson, Geoffrey H. Hartman, Frank Kermode, Frank Lentricchia, J. Hillis Miller, Edward Said. Derrida declined to offer an interpretation of the poem.

2. Cf. Williams' purportedly ultra-empiricist poetics: "We catch a glimpse of something, from time to time, which shows us that a presence has just brushed past us, some rare thing. For a moment we are dazzled. What was that? We can't name it; we know it never gets into any recognizable avenue of expression. *It is actually there, in the life before us, every minute that we are listening, a rarest element, not in our imaginations but there, there in fact.* It is that essence which is hidden in the very words which are going in at our ears. . ." (italics mine). See *The Autobiography of William Carlos Williams* (New York: Random House, 1951), pp. 360,362.

BIBLIOGRAPHY

STEVENS

The Collected Poems. New York: Alfred A. Knopf, 1954.

Letters of Wallace Stevens. Selected and edited by Holly Stevens. New York: Alfred A. Knopf, 1981.

The Necessary Angel: Essays on Reality and the Imagination. New York: Vintage Books, 1951.

Opus Posthumous. Ed. S.F. Morse. New York: Alfred A. Knopf, 1957.

The Palm at the End of the Mind. Ed. Holly Stevens. New York: Alfred A. Knopf, 1967.

Sur Plusieurs Beaux Sujets: Wallace Stevens' Commonplace Book. Ed. Milton J. Bates. Stanford, California: Stanford University Press, 1989.

Souvenirs and Prophecies: The Young Wallace Stevens. Ed. Holly Stevens. New York: Alfred A. Knopf, 1977.

OTHERS

Abrams, M.H. *Natural Supernaturalism: Tradition and Revolution in Romantic Literature*. New York: Norton, 1973.

Adorno, Theodor. *Aesthetic Theory*. Trans. C. Lenhardt. London: Routledge and Kegan Paul, 1984.

Arnold, Matthew. *Poetry and Criticism*. Ed. Dwight Culler. Boston: Houghton Mifflin, 1961.

Axelrod, Steven Gould S., and Helen Deese, eds. *Critical Essays on Wallace Stevens*. Boston: G.K. Hall, 1988.

Bachelard, Gaston. *On Poetic Imagination and Reverie*. Trans. Colette Gaudin. New York: Bobbs-Merrill, 1971.

Barnes, Julian. *New York Review of Books,* (9 Nov. 1989), pp.7-11.

Bates, J. Milton. *Wallace Stevens: A Mythology of Self*. Berkeley: University of California Press, 1985.

Baudelaire, Charles. *Selected Verse*. Trans. Francis Scarfe. Harmondsworth, Middlesex: Penguin, 1961.

Becker, George J., ed. *Documents of Modern Literary Realism*. Princeton. N.J.: Princeton University Press, 1963.

Beckett, Samuel. *Three Novels: Molloy, Malone Dies, The Unnamable*. New York: Grove Press, 1987.

Belamou, Michel. *Wallace Stevens and the Symbolist Imagination*. Princeton, N.J.: Princeton University Press, 1972.

Bellow, Saul. *Dangling Man*. New York: Signet Books, 1965.

Benziger, James. *Images of Eternity: Studies in the Poetry of Religious Vision from Wordsworth to T.S. Eliot*. Carbondale, Ill.: Southern Illinois University Press, 1962.

Bergonzi, Bernard. "The Sound of a Blue Guitar." In *The Critical Heritage*, ed. Doyle.

Bevis, William W. *Mind of Winter: Wallace Stevens Meditation, and Literature*. Pittsburgh, Pa.: University of Pittsburgh Press, 1988.

Blackmur, R.P. "Examples of Wallace Stevens." In *Stevens: The Critical Heritage*, ed. Doyle.

Blanchot, Maurice. *L' Espace Littéraire*. Paris: Gallimard, 1955.

Bloom, Harold. *Agon: Towards a Theory of Revisionism*. New York: Oxford University Press, 1982.

_____. *Wallace Stevens: The Poems of Our Climate*. Ithaca, N.Y.: Cornell University Press, 1977.

_____. *Ruin the Sacred Truths: Poetry and Belief from the Bible to the Present*. Cambridge, Mass.: Harvard University Press, 1989.

_____. ed. *Wallace Stevens: Modern Critical Views*. New York: Chelsea House, 1985.

Bornstein, George. *Transformations of Romanticism in Yeats, Eliot, and Stevens*. Chicago: University of Chicago Press, 1976.

————. ed. *Romantic and Modern: Revaluation of Literary Tradition*. Pittsburg: Pa.: Pittsburg University Press, 1977.

Borroff, Marie, ed. *Wallace Stevens: A Collection of Critical Essays*. Englewood Cliffs, N.J.: Prentice-Hall, 1963.

Bradbury, Malcolm, and James McFarlane, eds. *Modernism: 1890-1930*. Harmondsworth, Middlesex: Penguin, 1976.

Bradley, F.H. *Appearance and Reality: A Metaphysical Essay*. London: Oxford University Press, 1969.

Brazeau, Peter. *Parts of a World: Wallace Stevens Remembered*. New York: Random House, 1983.

Brogan, Jacqueline Vaught. *Stevens and Simile: A Theory of Language*. Princeton, N.J.: Princeton University Press, 1986.

Brown, Ashley and Robert S. Haller, eds. *The Achievement of Wallace Stevens*. New York: Lippincott, 1962.

Brown, Merle E. *Wallace Stevens: The Poem as Act*. Detroit: Wayne State University Press, 1970.

Burke, Kenneth. "William Carlos Williams: Two Judgments." In *Williams: A Collection of Critical Essays*, ed. Miller.

Bush, Ronald. *T.S. Eliot: A Study in Character and Style*. New York: Oxford University Press, 1985.

Cambon, Glauco. *The Inclusive Flame: Studies in Modern American Literature*. Bloomington, Ind.: Indiana University Press, 1981.

Carroll, Joseph. *Wallace Stevens' Supreme Fiction: A New Romanticism*. Baton Rouge: Louisiana State University Press, 1987.

Cassirer, Ernst. *An Essay on Man: An Introduction to a Philosophy of Human Culture*. Garden City, N.Y.: Anchor Books, 1953.

Chiari, Joseph. *Symbolism from Poe to Mallarmé: The Growth of a Myth*. New York: Gordian Press, 1970.

Coleridge, Samuel Taylor. *Biographia Literaria*. Ed. George Watson. New York: Dutton, 1956.

Collins, James. *The Existentialists: A Critical Study*. Chicago: Gateway Books, 1964.

Coyle, Reverly. *A Thought to be Rehearsed: Aphorism in Wallace Stevens's Poetry*. Ann Arbor, Michigan: UMI Research Press, 1983.

Danto, Arthur C. *Nietzsche as Philosopher*. New York: Macmillan, 1965.

Davie, Donald. *Pound*. London: Fontana Books, 1975.

_____. "On Stevens' Prolixity." In *Stevens: The Critical Heritage*, ed. Doyle.

Derrida, Jacques. *Writing and Difference*. Trans. Alan Bass. Chicago: Chicago University Press, 1978.

Doggett, Frank. *Stevens' Poetry of Thought*. Baltimore, Md.: Johns Hopkins Press, 1966.

_____.and Robert Buttel, eds. *Wallace Stevens: A Celebration*. Princeton, N.J.: Princeton University Press, 1980.

Donoghue, Denis. *Reading America: Essays on American Literature*. New York: Knopf, 1987.

_____. "For a Redeeming Language." In *Williams: A Collection of Critical Essays*, ed. Miller.

Doyle, Charles, ed. *Wallace Stevens: The Critical Heritage*. London: Routledge and Kegan Paul, 1985.

Ehrenpreis, Irvin, ed. *Wallace Stevens: A Critical Anthology*. Harmondsworth, Middlesex: Penguin, 1972.

_____. "Strange Relation: Stevens' Nonsense." In *A Celebration*, ed. Doggett and Buttel.

A Cure of the MInd

Eliot, T.S. *Anabasis: A Poem by St-John Perse*. New York: Harcourt, Brace, 1949.

_____.*Four Quartets*. London: Faber and Faber, 1970.

_____. *On Poetry and Poets*. New York: Farrar, Strauss and Cudahy, 1957.

Ellmann, Richard. *a long the riverrun: Selected Essays*. Harmondsworth, Middlesex: Penguin, 1989.

_____."Wallace Stevens' Ice-Cream." *In Aspects of American Poetry*, ed. Ludwig.

Ellmann, Richard, and Charles Feidelson, Jr., eds. *The Modern Tradition: Backgrounds of Modern Literature*. New York: Oxford University Press, 1965.

Emerson, Waldo Frank. *The Portable Emerson.* Ed. Carl Bode and Malcolm Cowley. Harmondsworth, Middlesex: Penguin, 1983.

Filreis, Alan. *Wallace Stevens and the Actual World*. Princeton, N.J.: Princeton University Press, 1991.

Fischer, Ernst. *The Necessity of Art: A Marxist Approach*. Harmondsworth, Middlesex: Penguin, 1963.

Flaubert, Gustave. *Correspondence*, II. Paris: Gallimard, 1980.

Fletcher, John Gould. "The Revival of Aestheticism." In *The Critical Heritage*, ed. Doyle.

Frankenberg, Lloyd. *Pleasure Dome: On Reading Modern Poetry*. Boston: Houghton Mifflin, 1949.

Frings, Manfred S., ed. *Heidegger and the Quest for Truth*. Chicago: Quadrangle Books, 1968.

Frisby, David. *Fragments of Modernity: Theories of Modernity in the Work of Simmel, Kracauer and Benjamin*. Cambridge: Polity Press, 1985.

Frye, Northrop. *Anatomy of Criticism: Four Essays*. New York: Atheneum, 1967.

_____. "The Realistic Oriole: A Study of Wallace Stevens." In *Stevens: A Collection of Critical Essays*, ed. Borroff.

Gardner, W.H., and N.H. MacKenzie, eds. *The Poems of Gerald Manley*. Hopkins. London: Oxford University Press, 1967.

Gelpi, Albert, ed. *Wallace Stevens: The Poetics of Modernism*. Cambridge: Cambridge University Press, 1985.

_____."Stevens and Williams: The Epistemology of Modernism." In *The Poetics of Modernism*, ed. Gelpi.

Gide, André. *The Fruits of the Earth*. Harmondsworth, Middlesex: Penguin, 1970.

Hamburger, Michael. *The Truth of Poetry: Tensions in Modern Poetry from Baudelaire to the 1960s*. Harmondsworth, Middlesex: Penguin, 1972.

Hartman, Geoffrey H. *Criticism in the Wilderness: The Study of Literature Today*. New Haven, Conn.: Yale University Press, 1980.

_____. *The Unmediated Vision: An Interpretation of Wordsworth, Hopkins, Rilke, and Valery*. New York: Harcourt, Brace, 1966.

Hassan, Ihab. "Imagination and Belief: Wallace Stevens and William James in Our Time," *The Wallace Stevens Journal*, 10 (1986): 3-8.

Heidegger, Martin. *Poetry, Language, Thought*. Trans. Albert Hofstadter. New York: Harper and Row, 1971.

Heller, Erich. *The Disinherited Mind: Essays in Modern German Literature and Thought*. Cambridge: Bowes and Bowes, 1952.

Hoffman, Frederick J. *The Mortal No: Death and the Modern Imagination*. Princeton, N.J.: Princeton University Press, 1964.

Holderlin, Friedrich and Eduard Mörike. *Selected Poems.* Transl. Christopher Middleton. Chicago: The University of Chicago Press, 1972.

Hough, Graham. *The Last Romantics*. London: Methuen, 1961.

Howe, Irving. "Another Way of Looking at the Blackbird." In *Stevens: The Critical Heritage*, ed. Doyle.

Hulme, T.E. *Speculations: Essays on Humanism and the Philosophy of Art*. Ed. Herbert Read. New York: Harcourt, Brace, 1924.

Jarrell, Randall. "Reflections on Wallace Stevens." In *The Critical Heritage*, ed. Doyle.

Jephcott, E.F.N. *Proust and Rilke: The Literature of Expanded Consciousness*. London: Chatto and Windus, 1972.

Josephson, Matthew. "An Extraordinary Personality." In *Stevens: The Critical Heritage*, ed. Doyle.

Joyce, James. *Stephen Hero*. Ed. Theodore Spencer. New York: New Directions, 1944.

_____.*Ulysses*, New York: Vintage Books, 1961.

Juhasz, Suzanne. *Metaphor and the Poetry of Williams, Pound, and Stevens*. Lewisburg, N.J.: Bucknell University Press, 1974.

Kahler, Erich. *The Disintegration of Form in the Arts*. New York: George Brazilier, 1968.

Kaufmann, Walter. *From Shakespeare to Existentialism*. Garden City, N.Y.: Anchor Books, 1960.

Kazin, Alfred. *An American Procession*. London: Secker and Warburg, 1985.

Kenner, Hugh. *A Homemade World: The American Modernist Writers*. New York: Knopf, 1975.

Kermode, Frank, ed. *Selected Prose of T.S. Eliot*. London: Faber and Faber, 1984.

_____.*The Sense of an Ending: Studies in the Theory of Fiction*. New York: Oxford University Press, 1967.

_____. "Dwelling Poetically in Connecticut." In *A Celebration*, ed. Doggett and Buttel.

Kessler, Jascha. "Wallace Stevens: Entropical Poet," *The Wallace Stevens Journal*, 1 (1977):82-86.

Knodel, Arthur J. *Saint John Perse: A Study of His Poetry.* Edinburgh: Edinburgh University Press, 1966.

Kremen, Kathryn R. *The Imagination of Resurrection: The Poetic Continuity of a Religious Motif in Donne, Blake, and Yeats.* Lewisburg: Bucknell University Press, 1972.

Kronick, Joseph G. "Large White Man Reading: Stevens' Genealogy of the Giant," *The Wallace Stevens Journal*, 7 (1983):89-98.

LaGuardia, David M. *Advance on Chaos: The Sanctifying Imagination of Wallace Stevens.* Hanover: University Press of New England, 1983.

Lawrence, D.H. *Reflections on the Death of a Porcupine and Other Essays.* Bloomington, Ind.: Indiana University Press, 1963.

_____. *The Rainbow.* London: Heinemann, 1963.

Leggett, B.J. *Wallace Stevens and Poetic Theory: Conceiving the Supreme Fiction.* Chapel Hill: University of North Carolina Press, 1987.

Lensing, George A. *Wallace Stevens: A Poet's Growth.* Baton Rouge: Louisiana State University Press, 1986.

Lentricchia, Frank. *After the New Criticism.* Chicago: The University of Chicago Press, 1980.

_____. *The Gaiety of Language: An Essay on the Radical Poetics of W.B. Yeats and Wallace Stevens.* Berkeley: University of California Press, 1968.

_____. *Modernist Quartet.* Cambridge, N.Y.: Cambridge University Press, 1994.

Leonard, J.S., and C.E. Wharton. *The Fluent Mundo: Wallace Stevens and the Structure of Poetry.* Athens, Georgia: The University of Georgia Press, 1986.

Levenson, Michael H. *A Genealogy of Modernism: A Study of English Literary Doctrine 1908-1922.* Cambridge: Cambridge University Press, 1990.

Lipking, Lawrence. *The Life of the Poet: Beginning and Ending Poetic Careers*. Chicago: The University of Chicago Press, 1976.

Litz, A. Walton. *Introspective Voyager*. New York: Oxford University Press, 1972.

_____. "Wallace Stevens' Defence of Poetry: 'La poésie Pure,' the New Romantic, and the Pressure of Reality." In *Romantic and Modern*, ed. Bornstein.

Lombardi, Thomas F. "Wallace Stevens and the Haunts of Unimportant Ghosts," *The Wallace Stevens Journal* 7 (1983): 46-53.

Ludwig, Richard M, ed. *Aspects of American Poetry*. Idaho: Ohio University Press, 1962.

McFarlane, James. "The Mind of Modernism." In *Modernism*: 189-1930, ed. Bradbury and McFarlane.

Mackey, Louis. "On Terms and Terminations: The Dissolution of Medieval Metaphor," *Texas Quarterly*, 21 (1978):80-88.

Macon, Eudo C. *Rilke*. London: Oliver and Boyd, 1963.

Mailer, Norman. "An Interview," *The Paris Review*, 31 (1964):28-58.

Mallarmé, Stéphane. *Poems*. Trans. Roger Fry, with an Introduction by Charles Mauron. New York: New Directions, 1951.

_____. *Selected Prose Poems, Essays and Letters*. Ed. Bradford Cook. Baltimore, Md.: Johns Hopkins Press, 1956.

Maritain, Jacques. *Creative Intuition in Art and Poetry*. New York: Meridian Books, 1955.

Mathiessen, F.O. *The Achievement of T.S. Eliot*. New York: Oxford University Press, 1972.

Miller, Henry. *Sexus*. New York: Grove Press, 1965.

Miller, J. Hillis. *Poets of Reality: Six Twentieth-Century Writers*. New York: Atheneum Books, 1969.

_____. ed. *William Carlos Willaims: A Collection of Critical Essays*. Englewood Cliffs, N.J.: Prentice Hall, 1966.

_____. "Stevens' 'Rock' and Criticism as Cure." In *Modern Critical Views*, ed. Bloom.

_____.*The Linguistic Moment: From Wordsworth to Stevens*. Princeton, N.J.: Princeton University Press, 1985.

_____."Theoretical and Atheoretical in Stevens." In *A Celebration*, ed. Doggett and Buttel.

Molina, Fernando. *Existentialism as Philosophy*. Englewood Cliffs, N.J.: Prentice-Hall, 1962.

Morris, Adelaide Kirby. *Wallace Stevens: Imagination and Faith*. Princeton, N.J.: Princeton University Press, 1974.

Nadeau, Maurice. *The Greatness of Flaubert*. Trans. Barbara Bray. LaSalle, Ill.: Open Court Publishing, 1973.

Nassar, Eugene Paul. *Wallace Stevens: An Anatomy of Figuration*. Philadelphia: University of Pennsylvania Press, 1965.

Newcomb, John T. *Wallace Stevens and Literary Canons*. Jackson, Miss.: University Press of Mississippi, 1992.

Nietzsche, Friedrich. *Philosophy and Truth: Selections from Nietzche's Notebooks of the Early 1870's*. Trans. Daniel Breazeale. Atlantic Highlands, N.J.: Humanities Press, 1979.

Ortega, José y Gasset. *History as System and Other Essays*. With an Afterword by John William Miller. New York: Norton, 1962.

_____.*The Modern Theme*. Trans. James Cleugh. New York: Harper Torchbooks, 1961.

_____. *The Dehumanization of Art and Other Writings on Art and Culture*. Garden City, N.Y.: Anchor Books, 1956.

Passmore, John. *A Hundred Years of Philosophy*. Harmondsworth, Middlesex: Penguin, 1968.

Pater, Walter. *Marius the Epicurean*. New York: The Modern Library, n.d.

_____.*The Renaissance: Studies in Art and Poetry.* With an Introduction by Kenneth Clark. London: Collins, 1964.

Pearce, Roy Harvey, and J. Hillis Miller, eds. *The Act of the Mind: Essays on the Poetry of Wallace Stevens.* Baltimore, Md.: Johns Hopkins Press, 1965.

_____.*The Continuity of American Poetry.* Princeton, N.J.: Princeton University Press, 1963.

_____. "Wallace Stevens: The Last Lesson of the Master." In *The Act of the Mind*, ed. Pearce and Miller.

_____."Toward Decreation: Stevens and the Theory of Poetry." In *A Celebration*, ed. Doggett and Buttel.

Perlis, Alan. *Wallace Stevens: A World of Transforming Shapes.* Lewisburg: Bucknell University Press, 1976.

Perloff, Marjorie. *The Poetics of Indeterminancy: Rimbaud to Cage.* Princeton, N.J.: Princeton University Press, 1981.

_____.*The Dance of the Intellect: Studies in the Poetry of the Pound Tradition.* Cambridge: Cambridge University Press, 1985.

_____.*The Futurist Moment: Avant-Garde, Avant Guerre, and the Language of Rupture.* Chicago: The University of Chicago Press, 1986.

Peters, H.F. *Rainer Maria Rilke: Masks and the Man.* New York: McGraw-Hill, 1963.

Peterson, Margaret. *Wallace Stevens and the Idealist Tradition.* Ann Arbor, Mich.: UMI Research Press, 1983.

Poirier, Richard. *The Renewal of Literature: Emersonian Reflections.* New York: Random House, 1987.

_____.*Poetry and Pragmatism.* Cambridge, Mass.: Harvard University Press, 1992.

Poulet, Georges. *Studies in Human Time.* Trans. Elliot Coleman. Baltimore, Md.: The Johns Hopkins Press, 1956.

Pound, Ezra. *Selected Poems.* London: Faber and Faber, 1981.

Queneau, Raymond. *Exercises in Style*. Trans. Barbara Wright. New York: New Directions, 1981.

Quinones, Ricardo J. *Mapping Literary Modernism: Time and Development*. Princeton, N.J.: Princeton University Press, 1985.

Raymond, Marcel. *From Baudelaire to Surrealism*. London: Methuen, 1970.

Rehder, Robert. *The Poetry of Wallace Stevens*. New York: St. Martin's Press, 1988.

Richards, I.A., "A Poetics of Tension." In *Literary Criticism*, ed. Wimsatt and Brooks.

Riddel, Joseph. *The Clairvoyant Eye: The Poetry and Poetics of Wallace Stevens*. Baton Rouge: Louisiana State University Press, 1965.

Rilke, Maria Rainer. *Selected Poetry*. Trans. Stephen Mitchell, with an Introduction by Robert Haas. London: Pan Books, 1987.

Rogueiro, Helen. *The Limits of Imagination: Wordsworth, Yeats, and Stevens*. Ithaca, N.Y.: Cornell University Press, 1976.

Rosenthal, M.L. "Stevens as Hedonist, Pluralist and Platonist." In *Stevens: The Critical Heritage*, ed. Doyle.

Ruland, Richard, and Malcolm Bradbury. *From Puritanism to Postmodernism: A History of American Literature*. London: Routledge, 1991.

Salusinszky, Imre. *Criticism in Society: Interviews*. New York and London: Methuen, 1987.

Sampson, Theodore. *Crispin's Voyage: The Search for a Vital Center in the Poetry of Wallace Stevens*. Athens: 1992.

Santayana, George. *Scepticism and Animal Faith*. New York: Dover Publications, 1955.

_____. *Interpretations of Poetry and Religion*. New York: Harper Torchbooks, 1957.

Sartre, Jean-Paul. *The Psychology of Imagination*. Secaucus, N.J.: Citadel Press, n.d.

Sausay, George Stone. *The Penguin Dictionary of Curious and Interesting Words*. Harmondsworth. Middlesex: Penguin, 1986.

Schaum, Melita. *Wallace Stevens and the Critical Schools*. Tuscaloosa: University of Alabama Press, 1988.

Schwartz, Delmore. "In the Orchards of the Imagination." In *Stevens: The Critical Heritage*, ed. Doyle.

Schwartz, Sanford. *The Matrix of Modernism: Pound, Eliot, and Early Twentieth-Century Thought*. Princeton, N.J.: Princeton University Press, 1985.

Scott, Nathan A. *The Poetics of Belief: Studies in Coleridge, Arnold, Pater, Santayana, Stevens and Heidegger*. Chapel Hill: University of North Carolina Press, 1985.

Scott, Stanley J. "Wallace Stevens and Williams James: The Poetics of Experience," *Philosophy and Literature*, 1 (1977):183-91.

Schneidau, Herbert N. *Ezra Pound: The Image and the Real*. Baton Rouge: Louisiana State University Press, 1969.

Shaviro, Steven. "'That Which Is Always Beginning': Stevens' Poetry of Affirmation." In *Critical Essays on Wallace Stevens*, ed. Axelrod and Deese.

Shelley, Percy Bysshe. *Shelley's Prose*. Ed. David Lee Clark. Albuquerque: University of New Mexico Press, 1954.

Smith, F. Joseph. "In-the-World and On-the-Earth: A Heideggerian Interpretation." In *Heidegger and the Quest for Truth*, ed. Frings.

Spender, Stephen. *The Struggle of the Modern*. London: Hamish Hamilton, 1963.

Stallknecht, Newton P. "Absence in Reality: A Study in the Epistemology of the Blue Guitar," *The Kenyon Review*, 21 (1959):545-562.

Stein, Gertrude. *Selected Writings*. Edited, with an Introduction and Notes, by Carl Van Vechten. New York: The Modern Library, 1962.

Steiner, George. *Language and Silence*. Harmondsworth, Middlesex: Penguin, 1969.

Sukenick, Ronald. *Wallace Stevens: Musing the Obscure*. New York: New York University Press, 1967.

Sypher, Wylie. *Loss of the Self in Modern Literature*. New York: Vintage Books, 1964.

_____. *Rococo to Cubism in Art and Literature*. New York: Vintage Books, 1963.

Tompkins, Jane P, ed. *Reader-Response Criticism: From Formalism to Post-Structuralism*. Baltimore, Md.: The Johns Hopkins University Press, 1980.

Valery, Paul. *Dialogues*. Trans. William McCausland Stewart, with Two Prefaces by Wallace Stevens. London: Routledge and Kegan Paul, 1957.

_____. *The Art of Poetry*. With an Introduction by T.S. Eliot. New York: Vintage Books, 1961.

_____. *Monsieur Teste*. Trans. Jackson Matthews. Princeton, N.J.: Princeton University Press, 1965.

Vendler, Helen. *On Extended Wings: Wallace Stevens' Long Poems*. Cambridge, Ma.: Harvard University Press, 1969.

_____. *Wallace Stevens: Words Chosen Out of Desire*. Knoxville: University of Tennessee Press, 1984.

_____. *Part of Nature, Part of Us: Modern American Poets*. Cambridge, Mass.: Harvard University Press, 1981.

Wagner, C. Ronald. "Wallace Stevens: The Concealed Self," *The Wallace Stevens Journal*, 12 (1988):83-101.

Walker, David. *The Transparent Lyric: Reading and Meaning in the Poetry of Stevens and Williams*. Princeton, N.J.: Princeton University Press, 1984.

Whitman, Walt. *Leaves of Grass and Selected Prose*. Ed. Scully Bradley. New York: Holt, Rinehart and Winston, 1966.

Widle, Jean T., and William Kimmel, eds. *The Search for Being: Essays from Kierkegaard to Sartre on the Problem of Existence*. New York: Noonday Press, 1962.

Williams, Carlos William. *Selected Essays*. New York: Random House, 1954.

_____. *Autobiography*. New York: Random House, 1951.

_____. *Paterson*. New York: New Directions, 1963.

Wimsatt, William K., and Cleanth Brooks. *Literary Criticism: A Short History*. New York: Knopf, 1957.

Winn, Ralph B., ed. *A Concise Dictionary of Existentialism*. New York: The Philosophical Library, 1960.

Yeats, William Butler. *A Vision*. London: Macmillan, 1962.

INDEX